--- Big Profits Small Effort ---

*YOUR **FAST TRACK** INTO THE WORLD OF **DIGITAL MARKETING***

*YOUR **FAST TRACK** INTO THE WORLD OF **DIGITAL MARKETING***

Copyright © Island Fuse Group 2019

All rights reserved.

ISBN: 9781791533083

The publisher has made every effort to ensure that the content of this book was accurate at the time of publishing. The content of this publication should not be reproduced, shared or transmitted in any form, whether electronically, mechanically and/or otherwise without prior written permission from the publisher. This book may not be lent, resold, hired or otherwise disposed of, without the prior consent of the publisher.

--- Big Profits Small Effort ---

YOUR **FAST TRACK** INTO THE WORLD OF **DIGITAL MARKETING**

- *Locate customers and help them to find you.*
- *Increase your ranking on search engines*
- *Position you and your business as go-to experts*
- *Automate your sales process*
- *Build a strong relationship with customers*
- *Gain a strong overview of digital marketing*

and much more…

By
Karla Ashley

Contents

1. Introduction	1
2. The Sales Funnel	5
3. Intelligent Websites	12
4. Increase visibility on search engines	23
36 SEO tactics	25
Content and Blogging	30
Pay Per Click (PPC)	36
5. Google is King	39
Google My Business	39
Google Search Engine	40
Google AdWords	41
Google Re-Marketing	41
Google Maps	42
Google Analytics	43
Google Trusted Stores	43
Google Shopping	44
Google Alerts	44
6. Connect on social media	46
14 tactics to grow your following	50
Facebook	55
Twitter	58
Youtube	59

Instagram	63
LinkedIn	66
Pinterest	69
Blogging sites (Tumblr/ Blogger/ Wordpress)	70
7. Mobile Technology	**73**
Periscope/ Meerkat (Video streaming apps)	73
Snapchat	75
Mobile Messenger Apps	75
Text Message Marketing	77
8. Effective Email Marketing	**82**
Increasing your open rate (OR)	87
1. Subject line	87
2. Personalisation	89
3. Appearance and Content	90
4. Call-to-action	93
9. Landing Pages	**97**
10. Retaining customers	**100**
Understanding customers	100
Loyalty schemes	102
Going the extra mile	102
11. Referrals and Reviews	**104**
12. Get free publicity	**107**
13. The future of Digital Marketing	**111**
Loss of Anonymity	111

Sharing Economy	112
Business Alliances	112
Mobile Technology	113
Algorithms	113
Voice Technology	114
The law	114
14. Conclusion	**116**
15. References	**119**
Books	119
Videos	120
Websites	120

Acknowledgements

I wish to express a big thank you to family and friends who were patient to bear with the commitment and isolation required to complete this work. I extend a special thank you to Dr. Shiela Wright and Dr. Robert Bradshaw who first encouraged me, many years ago, to publish my work. A big thank you Dr. Henry Mumbi, whose inspiration, support and knowledge has been invaluable. I would also like to express my appreciation to all the businesses I have worked for and with over the years, who have helped me to grow in this area of expertise. In particular, VeriVide Ltd, who gave me my first lead marketing position in 2002.

How to contact the author:
Karla Ashley

contact@rankabsolute.com

1. Introduction

Do you need to raise brand awareness? Are you struggling to draw prospects to your website or social media platforms and convert them into customers? Do you have a limited marketing budget? Do you simply wish to gain an understanding of digital marketing? Whether you are an established business owner, starting an enterprise, a marketing /sales professional or a student; if you have answered yes to any of these questions, then this is the book for you. This quick read is your fast track into the world of digital marketing.

It amazes me how many people are still apprehensive about digital marketing. Many people are intimidated by their lack of knowledge in this subject area and have tried to avoid it to the best of their ability, committing only to the minimum. So caught up in the everyday rigmarole of *"business as usual"* that they have not taken the time to recognise the changes in their business environment.

When a new technological trend hits the market those who are not up-to-speed to foresee and plan for them are usually left stupefied and undecided as to how and whether or not to adapt. By which time, those who invest in research and development and pay close attention to the tech-world, are more savvy to change and readily able to implement new processes. It's time for you to get a grip on digital marketing. The internet has already taken over the world and is about to shift into a higher gear. According to Jones: *"Nowadays, the internet is the first place people go to for information on almost anything they want to buy"*... *"you can reach more people, sell more things and find out more about customers so you can entice them to buy even more from you"* (Graham Jones, 2015).

Digital marketing is not as intimidating or complex as you may think. Like anything else it just requires a little know-how, strategy and application. If you are from a traditional marketing or sales background, many of the principles and techniques you already use can also be applied to digital marketing. Those who are equipped with even a basic awareness have found digital marketing to be an inexpensive, effective means to identify prospect customers, connect with them and convert them into repeat customers.

We have simplified and demystified the world of digital marketing and online sales conversion, equipping you with proven, tried techniques. We break down the main areas – search engine optimisation, blogging, social media, Google, mobile technology, email marketing and landing pages, into very practical, easy to digest portions. During the course of reading this book you will be on the edge of your seat, eager to implement the steps we outline, to see immediate results; asking yourself one question - *"Why didn't I do this earlier?"*

In chapter 2. we take you through the sales funnel model, helping you to examine your overall process of raising awareness and converting leads into sales. Here you will be able to take an overall look at your operations, reviewing methods you currently use and exploring additional methods you could implement to strengthen your sales process. Chapter 3. provides you with 28 proven tactics to improve the functionality of your website. No matter how wonderful your website is, we guarantee that there are ways to increase its level of sales conversion and competitive edge. Chapter

4. provides you with 36 tactics to increase your visibility on search engines, we also explain how blogging can help to position you and your business as experts and leaders within your niche. Chapter 5. is dedicated to Google, one of the world's leading technology giants; A key element to every marketing strategy, with services such as Google My Business, Google AdWords and Google Analytics. Chapter 6. provides you with a summary of the leading social media platforms (Facebook, Twitter, Instagram, LinkedIn, Pinterest, Youtube and Tumblr). An overview of their functionality, ways to grow your following and ways each unique platform can be used to help your business. Chapter 7. takes a look at the growing importance of mobile technology, how mobile messenger apps are outperforming social media platforms, as well as ways to incorporate text message marketing into your campaign activities. We help you to embrace email marketing in chapter 8, leveraging its huge, under-utilised and often under-estimated capabilities; The remaining chapters provide you with techniques to retain customers, gain positive referrals, reviews and free publicity, followed by an outlook of future developments that are likely to revolutionise the way we do business in the coming months and years.

This book will show you how to maximise your time, strategically laying out synchronised campaigns with automated messages, so that when you are not physically working, your business is still working for you. We provide you with techniques to monitor your digital performance against your return on investment (ROI), constantly adjusting to enhance your performance, identifying and eliminating what is not working for you and placing more emphasis on what works well. We show you how to gain warm sales leads, opposed to conducting embarrassing, painstaking, disappointing cold campaigns that generate cold leads. You will see many references to Google, not due to any deliberate bias, but instead, as a testament to their scope and influence in the digital sphere.

Should you desire to put into practice the strategies we highlight throughout this book we have 260 Resourceful Websites with free and for-purchase services that will help you to develop and manage your contact database, schedule and automate your email campaigns, analyse and measure your website and social media performance, boost your SEO, test the technical correctness of your website and so much more. This list is available free of cost from our website *(see list of Resourceful Websites at RankAbsolute.com/link.)*

Your fast track into the world of digital marketing

2. The Sales Funnel

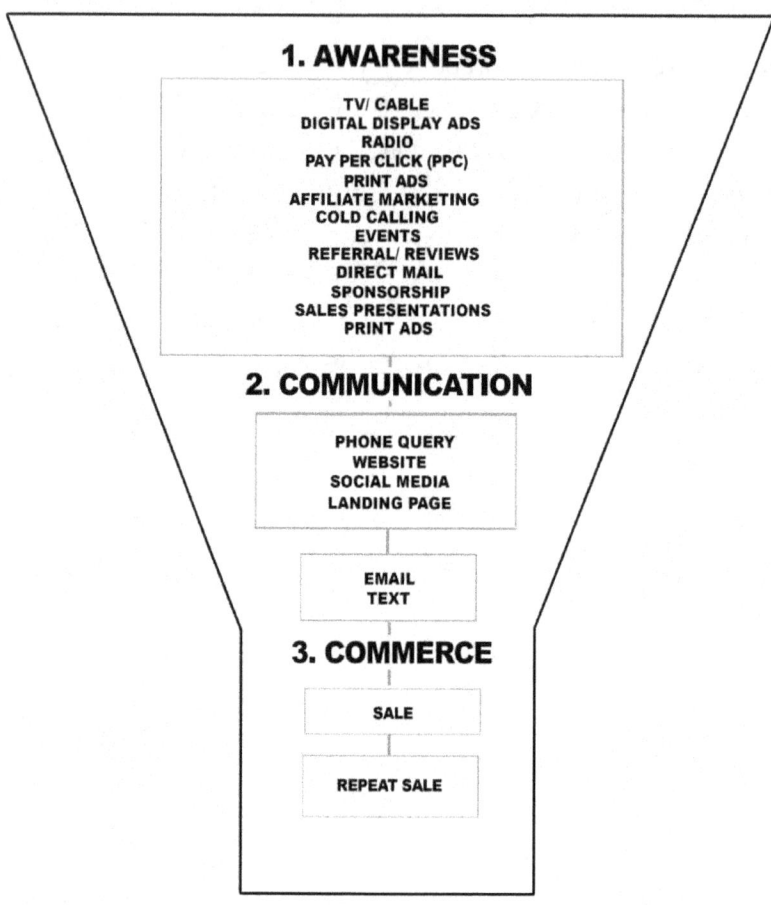

Fig 1. The Sales Funnel

The sales funnel forms the basis of our overall discussion on digital marketing. After all, what is the point of learning the digital strategies highlighted throughout this book, if the overall objective is not conversion. The sales funnel is a business road map to acquiring sales. Every business has a sales funnel, some more effective than others. Each sales funnel has some form of media used to generate awareness of the business, its products or services, a means of communication between the business and its prospects and merchant capabilities that ultimately generates sales. There is no ideal rate of sales conversion. The satisfactory rate depends on the individual business, according to their expectations, return on investment (ROI), competition, amongst other factors.

The sales funnel presented in Fig 1. demonstrates the overall structure and sequence of interaction from initial contact to repeat sales. This is a fairly comprehensive sales funnel. Not all steps or actions are necessary for all businesses. Some businesses may not take part in direct mail, cold calling, or affiliate marketing to generate leads. Some businesses may not even require the ability to facilitate phone queries, as such is the case with many online businesses. At each step of the sales funnel prospect customers will be lost for one reason or another. According to Jones: *"A typical webpage has a conversion rate of 2 per cent - that means 2 in every 100 people click through to find out more about a product. Then, once they have the information, an average of 2 per cent click on the 'buy now' button. However, for email marketing the conversion rates are much higher. Conversion rates on emails can be as high as 20 per cent - sometimes higher in some specific sectors"* (Graham Jones, 2015). Email marketing will be discussed more extensively in chapter 8.

The concept of a funnel, an instrument with a wide opening that gradually narrows towards the exit, used to shift content from the wide end through to the narrow end, suggests that substance (in this case - prospect clients) are either lost along the way or trickle down in smaller portions as they pass through the funnel. Some psychology, specialist skills and tactics are required throughout the process to increase the sale funnel's level of success. For example, understanding what motivates your prospects to take a desired action. If your sales funnel is ineffective, there are a number of issues that could be wrong with your marketing mix - product, price, place, promotion, people, processes, or physical evidence, (Booms & Bitner, 1981), inadvertently you could have all the right tools in place, yet lack the skills and tactics to execute them successfully.

One such example is a clothes manufacturer who developed a high quality brand that they were confident in. Keeping their overheads low with a small team, they were excited about the many inexpensive digital means they could use to exploit their brand. Yet they struggled with sales over the years. Months would go by with them receiving a couple sales orders. Barely managing to cover expenses, they attributed their poor performance to the decline of the textiles industry and the fact that their brand was fairly new to the market. They became so caught up with the day-to-day activities of trying to push products that they didn't investigate their suspicions further to gain a more solid understanding of their market place. Here are a few of the activities they engaged in and how they may have been more effective, if they had a tactical, customer-orientated sales funnel.

- Without any investment in brand awareness, they wanted wholesalers to give up valuable shelf space in order to retail their unknown, high-end, luxury brand. Had they invested in building brand awareness, it may have been easier for wholesalers to push a new brand that already had some level of media or street buzz. Digital marketing is fairly inexpensive and would have provided a great avenue for them to generate significant awareness. Although some investment and a highly innovative marketing strategy would have been required.

- They saw well-established competitors retailing on Amazon and decided to do the same. They set up Amazon accounts and shipped large amounts of stock to Amazon FBA (Fulfilled by Amazon). They invested in pay per click (PPC) advertising via Amazon which enabled them to gain a high ranking on Amazon and search engine results pages (SERP) for specific key words. However, months went by and they hardly saw any sales on Amazon. Had they paid attention, they may have realised that Amazon customers are not easily persuaded by attractive photographs, discounted prices or seductive product descriptions. Instead they rely heavily on customer reviews to make purchasing decisions. Especially from vendors they do not know. Amazon shoppers considered products without reviews to be undesirable and highly suspicious. They may have remedied this by launching a seasonal sales promotion on Amazon and publicising this to their current customer base, who had already made purchases via their website and were happy with the products. This promotion would then generate reviews on Amazon that would, in turn, help prospects on Amazon to gain confidence in their products.

- They engaged in monthly email blasts to their network of 500 wholesalers. Their emails were very lengthy, highly self-indulgent, impersonal, loaded with attractive photos and product descriptions. Yet had they paid closer attention to the poor email opening rates (OR) and click through rates (CTR), they may have considered changing their email strategy. Logically, wholesalers are attracted to low risk products they can sell quickly at a profit. Had they been able to identify a genuine strategy to achieve this or were able to convince wholesalers that they could meet this demand, they may have been able to increase their email open rates (OR), click through rates (CTR) and ultimately sales conversion.

- Customers who had purchased their products were very pleased. Which enabled them to generate quite a few positive reviews on their website. But these reviews were not highly visible to new prospects who visited their website. Had they made these positive reviews more obvious to new prospects, this may have helped to alleviate any apprehension from new prospects who had never purchased their products.

- They had a presence on social media such as Facebook, LinkedIn and Instagram but these pages were very inactive and poorly maintained. Which, inadvertently, stated that they cared very little for their online community and were uninterested in making a connection with their network.

Their lack of interaction on social media also meant that they were losing out on access to a wider market.

- They invested a small amount of money in Google AdWords which enabled them to gain the number one position for certain key words and phrases on Google search engine, outperforming their competitors. This high ranking helped them to generate queries, but these queries did not translate into sales. Their poor performance in other areas of marketing had a knock-on effect on their ability to convert search engine leads into sales.

- They offered nonsensical random discounts on their website as bait, in an attempt to generate instant sales. This only succeeded in making them look desperate, developing an ineffective sales relationship with prospects who were now only interested in receiving discounted offers. This activity also meant that any seasonal promotions would be ineffective, as their prospects were now desensitised to their frequent promotional discounts.

By their activities it was clear to see that this manufacturing company was very proactive and desperately desired to acquire sales. But their one-track thinking blindsided them to the need to be tactical in their approach and the fundamental need to pursue genuine interest in their prospect customers. Thus causing them to be completely disconnected from their market. As one of the keys to successful sales Jarvis states: *"Help your customers achieve what they want and you will receive what you want."* (Jackie Jarvis, 2015). So no matter how proactive you are in adapting digital marketing as a means to increase your sales conversion, you are likely to be unsuccessful without a fully customer-orientated approach. In the following chapters we will be exploring various online digital strategies and how best you can adapt them to increase your sales conversion.

TAKE ACTION:

- *Develop your own sales funnel, listing all the media, marketing and merchant tools you require for your business.*

- *Identify at each stage of your sales funnel what information and interaction you will need, in order to engage with your prospects and convert them into customers.*

- *If you are uncertain as to what channels of communication your target audience use, you can employ questionnaires, focus groups or surveys to gather more information.*

3. Intelligent Websites

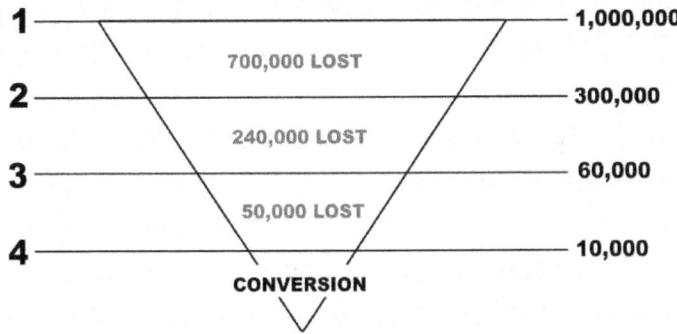

1. 1,000,000 prospects targeted through PPC, social media, email, etc. 700,000 prospects lost due to factors such as technical difficulty, slow loading speed, lack of mobile phone compatibility, being distracted by other activities or simply not interested.

2. 300,000 prospects progress to webpage. 240,000 prospects lost due to factors such as poor copywrite, auto-play content, poor design, complex colour schemes, poor navigations, boring generic content, distractions or loss of interest.

3. 60,000 are curious enough to stay on the webpage to find out more information. 50,000 prospects are lost due to factors such as being distracted, price sensitive or not interested in the product or service.

4. 10, 000 (2%) successful conversions. These prospects either provide their details or purchase a product or service.

Fig 2. Webpage Conversion Rate

Businesses are increasingly developing means to integrate their websites into their operations; connecting their social media networks, growing their email databases, fulfilling product orders, relieving the everyday stresses of their workforce through automated processes and ultimately saving money. Yet website technology is still very much underutilised by the vast majority of small and medium sized enterprises (SME's). Even more technologically advanced businesses such as Banks are aware that there is much more to leverage.

Not only have website capabilities evolved, but users too have become more sophisticated. Do you remember when we were mesmerised by flash animated intro sequences? Now we require far more to meet and exceed our expectations. After all, we have become spoilt by sites such as Amazon, with customised user experiences that track our every move and forecast our next, even before we do. Businesses that fail to grasp new technology and integrate more sophisticated user experience capabilities in the next two years, are risking their livelihoods, falling behind in this evolving digital world. Riding this tech-wave is not an option. Unfortunately the vast majority of SME's are nowhere near ready. If your website is still struggling to provide many of the following points, consider yourself a dinosaur on the verge of becoming extinct.

1. **Does your website quickly and effectively explain your business to your target audience?** Intelligent websites now achieve this with one downward scroll. This one downward scroll enables your website to provide a quick summary of your business, products, services and contact details.

2. **Is your website responsive and mobile friendly?** Another great fact about the downward scroll functionality is that it is mobile friendly, void of cumbersome navigations. Depending on your target demographics, up to 70% of website visitors are using mobile devices, opposed to a desktop computer. Mobile phones have smaller screens, making it more difficult to navigate, but much easier to scroll.

3. **What is the first impression your website conveys?** Whatever the reason users visit your website - to gain clarity, more information or purchase products and services, their first impression may be your only and last chance to engage that prospect. Having invested so much effort to get prospects to visit your website, it is essential to convey the right message. Visitors should instantly have a feel for your brand, be able to identify your products and services and ascertain what they are likely to expect if they do business with you.

4. **Do you use engaging, easy to read copywrite?** Your content must be appealing to your core target audience demographics - their likes, interests and lifestyle. Websites that are able to appease prospects, do so with a clear understanding of their psychological profile; Using the right words to paint pictures of their target audience's pain points, reassuring them as to how their products or services can meet their needs.

5. **Does your website have auto-play content?** This could be a music player or video that plays automatically when your webpage is opened. Such a feature can cause embarrassment for visitors if they are in an important meeting or a quiet

waiting area. Let your visitors decide if they wish to switch on your media player.

6. **Do you use effective images?** The right quality image can generate the desired response from prospects. It's often more effective to use images where humans are interacting with your products and services, opposed to an image of an empty office, or your product by itself. This will enable your site to be more relatable. According to Kourdi: *"...there is an old Chinese proverb that a says that one picture save 1,000 words and this is largely true"... "However, the simple fact is that everyone will look at the picture first, then read the words. It makes sense therefore to use pictures, diagrams and graphs whenever you can, to get your point across. These 'visual aids' always improve understanding and speed comprehension"* (Jeremy Kourdi, 2007). Be sure to use images for which you have the copyrights. There are many online stock photo sites where you can get free or for-purchase photos. We have listed several of these *(see list of Resourceful Websites at RankAbsolute.com/link)*.

7. **Does your website have video content?** Even more effective than static images or info-graphics, video content can convey your products and services in less than 30 seconds, with both audio and visual aids. A well-produced video can increase the amount of time visitors spend on your website, humanising the experience and helping you to build instant rapport. Videos can also be placed on multiple sites such as social media, aiding you to reach wider audiences.

8. **Does your website have strong SEO presence?** By optimising your website for search engines you will gain a higher ranking on search engine result pages (SERP). Leading more prospect customers to locate you online. We will discuss this further in chapter 4.

9. **Do you use complex colour schemes?** Complex or bright colours can bedazzle users into a state of chromostereopsis, leading to mental fatigue, frustration or even headaches. It is therefore best to use neutral colours that are less offensive.

10. **Do you use generic pop-ups?** The majority of internet users do not like pop-ups, but if your offer is creative and truly irresistible, users may be forgiving. Otherwise, the less irritated your users are, the better.

11. **Do you use live email address links?** This will make your website prone to attract email spam opposed to more secure email forms. With a professional email form you can collect all the necessary information you require from each query without providing your contact details. Thus saving you time, deterring deviant queries and empowering you to be selective about who you communicate with.

12. **Is it easy for prospect customers to recognise your website as being trustworthy?** Let prospect customers know that you are a trustworthy entity and that it is safe to do business with you. You can achieve this by adding industry awards, certificates and other accolades that can provide a sense of prestige, being established or indicate approval by a reputable 3rd party or industry authority. Let

your prospects know if you have been operating your business for many years, indicating that your business is established. An ssl certificate, signified by a padlock on your website, also lets customers know that their passwords, credit card details and other confidential information are safe on your website.

13. **Does your website offer anything distinct?** Offer something special that customers cannot get in-store. Highlighting that this offer is not available anywhere else, enables prospects to perceive your website as being exclusive, resourceful and worthwhile paying attention to.

14. **Does your website seamlessly integrate your social media platforms?** Social media platforms can be integrated into your website with widgets that users can interact with. Posting comments, likes, following and sharing, without having to leave your website. Your website is where you want prospects to spend time. Consider social media as mere tools to capture their attention.

15. **Does your website look distinct and attractive?** Many start-up businesses use website templates. However, search engines recognise generic templates and tend to penalise them. Prospects also view hundreds of websites, especially when researching a specific product or service. That's why it's important that your website stands out from the crowd. It is therefore worthwhile investing in a quality, unique, attractive website design.

16. **Are your terms and privacy policy up-to-date?** Update your terms and privacy policy according to gdpr regulations. Let users know what their data (name, image, bank details, email address, IP address, passwords, etc) will be used for, if they visit your website, subscribe to your mailing list or make a purchase. This should include data captured via cookies. Regulations online are becoming more stringent, so it's important to take these precautions. Your openness and transparency about your activities will help to establish trust with website users.

17. **Does your website grab audience's attention?** Some distractions and movements are useful to grab audience's attention, especially within the first 2 seconds. Make images and/or info-graphics on your website dynamic. If an image changes within the first 2 - 3 seconds of a visitor viewing your webpage, they may stay another 2 seconds to see if more interesting information is presented to them, or be curious enough to click on another page.

18. **Does your website load quickly?** Unless you have something irresistible that audiences are eager to see, any website that takes too long to load is likely to lose visitors instantly. Visitors will either click away, be distracted by a conversation, their phone may ring, an instant message alert may appear, or their train may arrive at their final destination. There are many distractions for websites to contend with. So don't put your website at a disadvantage with a slow loading speed. This is discussed further in chapter 4.

19. **Do you have an effective landing page?** A landing page is a page designated to capture leads for a campaign. This page will have a specific lead magnet (free giveaway) that drives prospects to make a purchase or to submit their data (e.g. email address or name) through an online form. This is discussed further in chapter 9.

20. **Are mobile messenger apps integrated into your website?** If you have not already done so, it's high time you do. Mobile messenger apps such as WhatsApp are leading the way, outperforming social media in terms of users and responsiveness. This will be discussed further in chapter 7.

21. **Do you drive prospect customers away with external links?** Don't allow external links, such as social media pages, to drive prospects away from your website. Ensure that your live links open in a separate window. This increases the likelihood of prospects returning to your webpage once they have finished viewing the other link. The more prospects visit your website and the longer they stay, the more optimised your website will be for search engines.

22. **Do you up-sell on your website?** You can up-sell on your website in a similar way you would up-sell to a prospect customer at your place of business. Let prospects know what other solutions you have that may be appealing to them. Amazon is excellent at up-selling, placing additional accessories and complementary products at the point of purchase.

23. **How effective is your website at conversion?** Don't let visitors leave your website without accomplishing a desired activity, whether that is to leave their email address or make a purchase. This is achieved by adding a call-to action, such as *"sign up to our newsletter"*, *"book today for 20% discount"*, *"register now"*, or *"click here to download your free..."*

    Provide an incentive for visitors to submit their details. This will enable you to keep in touch and initiate the process of converting that prospect into a customer. Another great way to achieve this is to create a promotion with an offer that has scarcity and a time limit, e.g. *"only 200 copies, offer ends in 21 days"*. If visitors are simply leaving without you acquiring something, then your method of conversion may not be effective enough. It's time to implement more effective tactics to bring about greater conversion. This is discussed further in chapter 8.

24. **Do you promote your business alliances via your website?** You can add links to your business alliance's website. This helps to further solidify your alliance by promoting their business to your customers. In exchange, your alliance will promote your business on their website. Review the way your alliances are promoting your business, making alternative suggestions if there is anything you are unhappy with. Alliances can be built with businesses that have the same target audience demographics, but offer non-competing products or services.

25. **How effective are your key words and phrases?** Ensure you have researched your keywords and phrases to generate effective search engine results. More about this can be found in chapter 4.

26. **Do you have a blog?** Adding blogs to your website, with effective keywords and phrases can help to enhance your search engine presence. Quality blogs can also help to establish you as an expert and your business as an authority within a specific niche. More information can be found in chapter 4.

27. **Is your website updated frequently?** Search engine robots crawl websites frequently to identify new activities and review performance. Inactivity on your website, especially on your home page and other key pages, can give the impression that your website is not worthy of search engine traffic. This is discussed more in-depth in chapter 4.

28. **How intelligent is your website?** Websites have an incredible amount of potential. Some websites can detect when visitors are about to click away, or select the back button; triggering a pop-up to appear that tempts that visitor with an exclusive, one-time discount. Some websites greet visitors with an instant messenger, a real person who is ready to communicate with them 2 seconds after they open the home page. The more strategic, inbuilt capabilities your website has, with the ability to integrate seamlessly into your work processes, including monitoring stock inventory, customer relationship management (CRM), etc, and communicate this information across your entire

organisation, the more efficient and effective your operations will be. The capabilities of website technology are almost infinite. Internet users have a lot more choice, distractions and less time and money. Its within your best interest to identify ways to captivate their attention. Your website is a resourceful asset; leverage it to the best of your capabilities.

As mentioned previously according to Jones (2015) a webpage has a conversion rate of approximately 2 per cent, which is not the highest conversion rate. Nevertheless the website is a highly important marketing tool. It enables a business to present itself to the world and aids all other aspects of sales and marketing activities, whether that is to simply provide information or even to facilitate merchant activities.

TAKE ACTION:

- *Compare your website with each of the points listed above.*

- *Identify areas where your website can be improved and how these improvements can assist your level of sales conversion.*

- *Work with experienced web developers such as RankAbsolute.com to implement these developments.*

4. Increase visibility on search engines

Search engines are often the first protocol for online users when they have a question, are trying to locate a website or contemplating the purchase of a product or service. According to Jones *"One thing that is clear from the online world, however, is that the vast majority of sales journeys begin online. People are choosing cars and houses online, as well as more obvious purchases such as fashion"* (Graham Jones, 2015).

If your website is not prominent on search engine result pages (SERP) it will be difficult for prospects to find your website. The top 5 listed positions are the aspirations of any reputable business. But this position is becoming more difficult to attain because of increased competition. To legitimately achieve this high ranking without paying for advertising requires a long-term strategic investment. No one can guarantee how a search engine will rank your website, but a good technical strategy could give you an edge over your competition.

To initiate a search, words, phrases and questions are entered into a search engine search bar. With words being the decisive factor its critical for search engines to be able to anticipate what the user is likely to write and the kind of responses it needs to generate in order to match the most relevant answers to the search performed. The accuracy of words used by the internet user and the ability of search engine algorithms to match these words to the most appropriate content, will determine the effectiveness and accuracy of that search engine. Words are therefore the foundation of the whole search engine function. If you are able to foresee what likely words and phrases will be used and what search engines are likely to do with these words and phrases to generate results, you can optimise your website's search engine performance.

Search engine optimisation (SEO) is the method of increasing free organic traffic to your website. Algorithms are mathematical formulas used to generate calculated output(s), based on a specific or combination of input(s). There are many different types of algorithms with different functions. In the context of search engines, one algorithm may focus on spelling and grammar, another may identify clusters of key words and phrases and another may focus on quality backlinks. Google for instance has many different algorithm such as Google Mobile Friendly, Mobile Geddon, Panda, Penguin, Pigeon, Payday, Pirate, EMD (Exact Match Domain), Top Heavy and Hummingbird to name just a few. Whilst other search engines such as Bing have their own algorithms. The more fine-tuned and strategic your website is, the more effective it will engage with each algorithm.

Effective use of key words and phrases around any given topic will make your website easy for search engines to detect and rank. A basic way to identify key words and phrases is to brain storm them, and then test their effectiveness by entering them into search engines to compare the results generated. You can use your competitor's url to see how they are ranking and for what key words and phrases; identify and analyse the results of similar websites in the top 10 search results. We can also recommend websites that will help you to analyse your website's performance in a variety of other ways, such as identifying how many web users are visiting your website, how they are finding you and how much time they are spending on your website. *(see list of Resourceful Websites at RankAbsolute.com/link).*

36 SEO tactics

Below you will find a few tactics businesses use to increase their search engine performance:

1. Well **established websites** that have been online for a long time will have far better search results. This is because search engines have a historic reference of established websites, and their past performance provides assurance that they are likely to be around for some time to come. Whilst new, un-established websites, with very little history are likely to see fewer results and receive less support from search engines.

2. Having your **business listed** in online directories and industry trade directories, helps to increase your website ranking. All information should be consistent wherever your business is referred to or listed online. For example, if you use an international dialling code on your website, then use an international dialling code everywhere your phone number appears. If you use "Ltd" at the end of your business name, then use it everywhere your business name is mentioned or listed online. Do not abbreviate your business name unless you do so everywhere. This will create greater consistency, empowering search engines to identify your business as the same entity everywhere your business is listed.

3. Slow website **loading speed** is a hindrance for website users, especially those using mobile phones. There are a number of ways you can increase your website loading speed, these include using a content delivery network (CDN) - servers located closer to your users; Optimising your images by making sure they are sized correctly; Avoiding bad practices such as render-blocking java script and css; Enabling compression when delivering large files such as documents through your browser and allowing browser cashing so website visitors can save the memory of your webpage in their browser and go back to it later, opposed to re-loading your website each time.

4. As discussed in chapter 3. your website must be **easy to navigate** on mobile devices. The easier it is for visitors to navigate your website, the more likely it is for search engines to rank your website.

5. Use a quality, **reliable hosting company** to ensure that your website will not keep crashing, going offline or load pages slowly. Again this kind of interference is a big turn-off for website visitors and search engines tend to grant websites a lower ranking if they are not user-friendly.

6. Monitor your **key performance indicators (KPI)** such as **click through rates (CTR)** and **page views.** If you have adverts on your website you need to monitor **impressions** (how many times ads on your page are viewed), **ad sessions**, and where your traffic is coming

from, in order to identify what is working effectively for you. By analysing this information you can eliminate strategies that are not working and place greater emphasis on strategies that do work.

7. Make sure your **website is technically correct**. Poor url structure, broken page links, sub-domains, changing your domain name, re-designing, or even the way your website links and re-directs pages from a previous version, all affects your SEO performance; Causing issues such as 404 errors, which work against your search engine performance by creating a lot of technical confusion. Use clean urls, with words separated by hyphens. You can check for bad codes by entering your url into a W3C website validator. If you identify a lot of errors we recommend hiring a qualified expert such as RankAbsolute.com to clean your codes.

8. As mentioned briefly in chapter 3, your **website must be up-dated frequently** in order for search engines to consider it current and relevant. This can be achieved with an interactive comment section, new content, or even social media feeds. Search engine robots crawl websites frequently checking the site's performance - the amount of visitors, CTR, bounce rates, 404 errors, user engagement, etc. It's not only important to search engines that your site is updated frequently, but also visitors who have a genuine interest in your products or services.

CHAPTER 4: Increase visibility on search engines

9. **Bad SEO practices** could have serious repercussions for your website. Techniques that may have been effective at increasing your search engine presence in 2010, may not work now with more intelligent algorithms. It's important for you to keep up-to-date on these new developments or risk damaging your online presence. One such bad practice includes publishing the same article or blog to multiple websites. This activity will no longer increase your search engine results. As stated previously search engines hate repetition.

10. The use of **social media** can boost your SEO. Social media platforms naturally have superior inbuilt SEO capabilities. Social media pages with customised url, contact details of your business, live links to your website, a profile of your Director and other useful information can help to bring more attention to your website. This is discussed more in-depth in chapter 6.

11. Invest in **quality website language translation** for target markets overseas. This will help your website to gain key word ranking in foreign territories. Thus increasing traffic from prospects in those territories.

12. Although it might seem time-consuming, each product or service you offer should have its own webpage with **meta tags, key words, phrases and descriptions** to enable greater SEO.

13. Don't use too many **plugins, pop-ups and widgets** on your website. This will not only help to increase your

website loading speed, but also causes less irritation to users and ultimately make your website more search engine friendly.

14. Make sure your **website is on https** so that your website is secure with an ssl certificate. Http (hypertext transfer protocol) is the most common way of connecting websites to servers, but it is not secure and can easily be intersected by hackers. However, https (the "s" meaning secure), is a protocol used for high-risk websites that carry sensitive customer data such as banks, guaranteeing a secure, encrypted connection.

15. Before registering a website **domain name**, perform background checks in case it was originally owned by spammers. Such a history can have bad ramifications for the future of your website.

16. **Navigation breadcrumbs** are often used on websites with many pages, some of which are hidden behind secondary pages. Navigation breadcrumbs give your website a big SEO boost, highlighting to users their location at all times, making your website navigations more clearly defined.

17. **Video website maps** on your website encourages search engines to recognise that your website has interesting, interactive video content. Not only can you add video site maps to your website, but you can also submit them to search engines.

Content and Blogging

The following techniques will enable you to enhance your SEO capabilities, through online content, specifically blogging; whether on your website, a social media platform such as Tumblr, Blogger, or even someone else's blog. Blogging is also a great way to promote your level of expertise throughout the World Wide Web. According to Jarvis: *"An expert is a person who has a high level of skill and knowledge in a particular area. Experts are often thought of as the best problem solvers, solution providers or thought leaders – their knowledge is trusted by others." ..."Promoting yourself as an expert is an excellent way to gain trust and recognition in your industry. Customers love experts and would rather pay more for the product or service from someone who is known as one of the best in the business."* (Jackie Jarvis, 2015). The following tips will enable you to create the most effective SEO blogs:

18. Create a lot of **lengthy (1000+ words),** high quality, and in-depth content; Covering as many angles around your subject as possible. Your content should focus on a niche topic, be so detailed, comprehensive and thorough that readers won't need to go elsewhere for information relating to the topic. Use words to paint pictures to enable your readers to understand what you are trying to communicate. Your content should flow well, be easy to read and structured logically for readers to follow.

19. **Don't stuff key words** throughout your content, adding them where they don't belong. Search engines can identify key word stuffing and they do not treat this

activity favourably. Search engines care about the quality of your content so ensure your text reads logically and naturally, using key words seamlessly throughout. A key word can be included in your url, heading, subheading and in the body of your text (once or twice). Deciding on an outline for your text initially will enable you to identify what sections will have what information and the most important words you need to include.

20. Search engines also check the quality of content based on **spelling and grammar**. It is therefore essential to ensure that your content is well-written.

21. Search engine robots ignore **generic content** with common, repetitive words that appear in too many articles of a similar nature. Instead they tend to search for more important, uncommon, distinct words in a similar context. If you only use common words and phrases, search engines will think that you are copying everyone else, thus penalising your content with a lower ranking.

22. Search engines do not read **images**. By adding images and info-graphics with alt text, meta tags and descriptions, you enable search engines to identify what your image is about, providing further evidence that your content is interesting.

23. Similar to images, search engines cannot watch **videos**, but they do recognise them as being interesting to

website users. Website users have short attention spans. Videos are interactive, with audio and visual content making them engaging. It is therefore important to optimise videos for search engines with titles, key words, phrases, meta tags, effective descriptions and transcripts. To transcribe your video you can use transcript software. The clearer the vocals, with little interference, background noise, or variations in dialect, the more precise your transcript will be. We can recommend transcript software *(see list of Resourceful Websites at RankAabsolute.com/link)*.

24. **Backlinks** are a form of cross-referencing that enables you to draw attention to your website. You can use external backlinks to influential websites and create internal links to content on your own website. If you are going to build links, make sure they are worthwhile. There is no point having links to websites that search engines are likely to ignore. Excessive use of low quality, irrelevant or non-related backlinks creates distrust from search engines. If search engines do not trust your content, they won't trust your website. Don't over-link. Your links should be relevant to readers and not just used for website ranking. Useful links can include backlinks to guest blogs on other websites associated with your industry, links to features, online directories, social media pages, membership sites, reputable press and online media, through editorial coverage and/or interviews. Network with other bloggers providing backlinks to their blogs. In turn they may reference and create backlinks to your content.

Quality backlinks from influential websites can significantly help your website to rank in search engines.

25. Your content could become a **featured snippet**, or what others describe as "rank zero" on Google if your content answers key search engine queries. Google hummingbird algorithm wants to answer user's queries. Featured snippets are an exclusive section displayed on Google search engine results pages (SERP), just below PPC adverts, but with a higher visibility than organic search results. This is discussed more extensively in chapter 5.

26. **Make your content personable**. You can achieve this through your tone of voice, speaking in first person narrative or sharing personal stories in the form of case studies to illustrate the points you are making. People like people they can relate to. Make your first paragraph very strong, in order to hook audiences, gets them curious and inspire them to read on. Also make your title eye-catchy, engaging, relevant and SEO friendly.

27. **Break up your content** to make it more interesting. You can achieve this by using bold headings, images, info-graphics, links, diagrams, videos, audio, italics, spaces between paragraphs, interactive and engaging forms and comments fields. Subheadings are useful, because they enable readers to skip to the sections they wish to read and extract the information that is most relevant to them. Ensure that your sentences are straight to the point, chatty, and interesting, yet professional.

CHAPTER 4: Increase visibility on search engines

28. **Brand your content** to make it easily recognisable at a glance, by adding your corporate colours, business logo, or even through your tone of voice. The greater the consistency you maintain across all communication associated with your business, the more effective your impact will be. Ensure that your name, business name and links to your website are included in your blog as a means to draw prospects to your website, promote your products, services and ultimately generate sales.

29. Use a **content calendar** to plan and schedule your content in advance. Your content should sync with relevant events, current affairs and complement your entire marketing efforts. Premeditate your end goal - the effect you want each article to have on readers and what action readers are likely to take as a result of reading your blog. Brain-storm and research topic ideas in advance to ensure there is significant scope to produce extensive content. How-to articles that answer questions tend to be effective. Identify key words, phrases and subject headings to organise your content. Write non-stop without editing, then finally review and edit your content.

30. **Don't procrastinate** the posting of your blogs by trying to make them perfect and precise. Accept that at the beginning you won't know everything or have all the skills and knowledge. Just focus on getting your content out. Write one, publish it and move on to the next. You can always re-visit your post to edit it once it has been published online. Constantly review your work and

study the work of others who are more successful and accomplished than you. Then implement the new techniques you discover to improve your work, developing your own formulae for success.

31. **Reference and quote** content that are not your own original ideas. Any idea you include from the works of others should be referenced as their work and not used as your own.

32. **Add a call-to-action** on your blog to gain useful information or a desired reaction from your readers. You can learn more about call-to-actions in chapter 8.

33. Be proactive by writing blogs for other websites. This is called "**guest blogging**". This gives you more control over the content and links you wish to share, enabling you to direct the narrative of your business. However, it's important to ensure that your blog matches the tone and content of the website you wish to publish on.

34. **Approach influencers** who blog online to promote your products and services. You can entice them with freebies, products, services or money. But be highly selective, to ensure your efforts are well spent. It's important to establish how well-known this influencer is, the strength of their social media following, what kind of reputation they have and if they share a similar target audience demographic.

35. You can **drive traffic** to your blog by posting links to them on social media, emailing them to your contact database and using PPC to drive traffic to them from search engines.

36. Focus on satisfying the needs of your **target audience** first. If you are successful in meeting their needs then SEO will naturally support your efforts.

Pay Per Click (PPC)

As mentioned briefly, PPC (pay per click) advertising is a short cut for gaining high SEO ranking. PPC is a form of advertising that is unique to the internet. In fact it is currently the standard model for advertising online. PPC, as the name suggests, is advertising you pay for when prospects click your ad. PPC services are made available by search engines such as Google, online stores such as Amazon and social media platforms such as Facebook. PPC is one of the most effective methods to draw traffic to your website, social media or any online page you wish to promote. It enables you to bypass a lot of the hard work of SEO to get your advert in prominent search engine results relating to your key words, depending on how much you spend (the bid amount) and how effective your advert is in generating clicks. PPC features your ad as a paid for advertisement in search engine result pages (SERP), in a section above other generically ranked search results for any given topic. The cost of PPC advertising can be relatively cheap, but varies according to factors such as the volume of bids for that key word and seasonal variations in demand.

PPC is the most precise targeted form of advertising that exists. You have the options to structure your campaign by key words, title, geographic location, language and budget, intermittently monitoring how much you are spending in real time. You can schedule your ad according to the times your business is open and the times your prospect customers are most active online. Initially you may wish to make your ad campaign quite general in terms of ad times and geographic reach, then analyse your campaign performance over the course of a month to see where your ad performed best. You can then choose to switch your ads off during periods your ads are less effective and narrow down your scope to the most responsive variables.

You can measure the success of your PPC campaigns through key performance indicators (KPI). KPI are performance variables that are measurable such as click through rates (CTR), impressions, page views, engagements, Ad sessions, newsletter subscriptions, surveys completed and return on investment (ROI). Whatever metrics are important to the successful performance of your PPC campaign.

Social media PPC may be the most effective at targeting, as your targeting can easily be narrowed down to specific groups according to their interest. For example you may be selling a bridal product and want to reach out to a specific group with an interest in that topic. On social media platforms you will be able to locate groups based on themes such as wedding, thus enabling direct targeting. It's important to ensure that your PPC ad clearly identifies what it is you are offering, otherwise persons with no interest in your products or services may be misled to click your add; thus costing you a financial loss.

The strength of your SEO rests entirely on the strength of your overall marketing strategy both online and offline. All your marketing activities should aggregate interest in your business, whether exhibitions, networking events, guest speaking, publicity stunts, traditional display ads, etc. The more proactive your business is and the more overall interests you generate, ultimately your search engine ranking will be enhanced.

TAKE ACTION:

- *Identify what key words and phrases are relevant to your business, products/services or industry.*

- *Using a public computer (e.g. library) search for these key words and phrases, identifying your business' ranking position for each, along with your competitor's ranking position.*

- *Having identified your ranking position for key words and phrases in search engines, device an action plan using the techniques highlighted in this chapter to increase your visibility for the search terms you deem relevant. Whether that strategy includes the use of PPC, blogging, backlinks, etc.*

5. Google is King

Google is one of the world's leading technology companies, providing over a hundred services ranging from hardware to software and the internet. Google services include headsets, watches, android, laptops, G-Suite (Google's equivalent to Microsoft Office 365), browser, cloud storage, search engine, social media network, Google Translate, Google Flight, Google Maps and so much more. Some of which have become seamlessly integrated into our everyday lives. Google owns Chrome, Youtube, a host of other brands and is set to monopolise tech completely. It can be described as professional suicide to omit Google from your marketing plan. We are going take a brief overview of a few Google services which are applicable to businesses and aiding the sales conversion process. These are namely - Google My Business, Google search engine, AdWords, Re-Marketing, Google Maps, Google Analytics, Google Trusted Stores, Google Shopping, Google Alerts and Local Inventory Ads. With news released from several official sources in 2018, stating that Google+ will be shutting down, we have decided to omit this platform from the following list.

For the sake of those reading this chapter in isolation and not wanting to be too repetitive, we have not included Youtube as it is discussed in chapter 6, where we take a more in-depth look at social media platforms.

Google My Business

As with many of Google's online services, Google My Business is free. It operates in a similar manner to a social media platform, enabling you to create a profile for your business with your business name, a photo or logo, opening hours, phone number, live links to your website, address with a map, business description, services, booking button for prospects to book your services direct, a messaging service so that prospects can contact you direct, a Q&A section, promotional videos, a website builder for companies without their own website and feeds from other social media platforms. Finally, a review section, where customers can review your services and add a star rating. This section is especially important for your business ranking on search engines. The more reviews your business receives, the more activity is highlighted on your profile, indicating to Google that your business is popular, thus increasing your search engine ranking.

Google Search Engine

Google's search engine is notably the world's largest. It's important to submit your url for indexing on Google. Only index pages that require prominent visibility. Google has several paid services that can help your business to gain more visibility on their search engine such as Google AdWords and Re-Marketing, these are discussed in more detail later in this chapter.

Google search engine has an exclusive feature called *"featured snippet"* or what others call *"zero listing"*. As mentioned in chapter 4, online content that is highlighted as featured snippets, are those that actually answer questions that search engine users are searching for. Google has an algorithm called hummingbird that is dedicated to locating the most accurate answers for user's queries.

Featured snippets are displayed on Google search engine results pages (SERP), just below PPC adverts, yet having a higher visibility than organic search results, in a larger, bold format. You can use your heading or subheadings to directly answer likely search engine queries to attain this exclusive feature. For example, if a search engine user asked the question - *"Where are the best clubs in London?"* Google will search for the website with the most relevant answer, such as - *"The best clubs in London are..."* It is therefore important to understand what kind of questions users are asking and directly answer those questions. If you are writing a review, use the word *"review"* in the heading to help users who are searching for *"reviews"*.

Google AdWords

AdWords is Google's pay per click (PPC) program. AdWords enables you to rank high on Google search results and for your adverts to appear on websites that participate in the Google AdSense program. Advertisers only pay when viewers actually click on their advert. Whilst the owner of the participating website receives payment each time a visitor clicks an advert displayed on their website. You can use PPC ads to drive prospects to your landing page, social media, blog or website. You can also link your Google AdWords account to your Google Analytic account to monitor your campaign performance.

Google Re-Marketing

Have you noticed products you may have viewed or taken a keen interest in on one website now appearing in adverts on other websites you visit and across different digital devices. That's because those select websites partner with Google AdSense in order to display Google adverts. Google re-marketing enables advertisers to take the PPC experience to another level, promoting products and services of interest to individuals after they have left the website. This heightened level of exposure for products and services through such a direct, repetitive manner creates greater familiarity for prospects. The idea is that repetition and exposure aids the purchase decision-making process and will increase the likelihood of a sale.

Google Maps

You can enable prospects to locate your business more easily by adding it to Google Maps. Many people use GPS navigation on Google Maps to locate places they are searching for. Bing and Apple also have their own version, notably Apple Maps and Connect. Google has added more features to their Map services enabling you to save your key locations such as home, work, family and friend's addresses. If these addresses are already listed in your phone, you can give Google access to your contacts and Google will import these addresses. You can share your location with your friends, family and even the public. You can change the time of day to find time specific events. For example if you select night you can find night life in your location. You can identify the best form of transport to get to and from destinations and the best route to avoid obstructions and heavy traffic. Through Google Street View, a feature on Google Maps, also accessible via search engine and Google My Business, you can offer prospects a virtual tour of your business online. It's a great way to be open and transparent with your prospects. From the comfort of their home they can see your premises then check your website to browse your products.

Google Analytics

Google Analytics provides you with information about your website's performance such as bounce rates, click through rates (CTR) and loading speed. You can find out how many prospects are visiting your website (unique or repeat), their demographics, the devices and browsers they are using, the various avenues through which they are finding your website, whether that be social media, direct, search engines, referral websites, PPC or even email. You can identify the most popular pages visited, how much time visitors are spending on your website, the activities they take part in such as watching videos, filling in forms or signing up to your newsletter.

Google Analytics also has further tools that enable you to identify and cross reference your data based on key performance indicators (KPI) and customise your reports. For example if you identify that women are making more expensive purchases on your website, you can cross reference different data to find out more about this market, such as their location and the time of day they are shopping. Based on such detailed information you can then design specific tailored advertising campaigns to target this market; Or if you identify that young adult males are making most of their purchases online, late in the evening, using their mobile phones. You may wish to display special tailored promotional offers for young men at that specific time of day and optimise your website to be mobile friendly.

Google Trusted Stores

Google Trusted Stores is a badge added to your website to indicate that it is secure. It is a free service designed to create greater trust and security online, in return this trust is likely to lead to greater sales conversion. Google's extension on your website will monitor shipment and confirmation feeds from your website to validate its level of trustworthiness. Google Trusted Stores offers buyers up to $1,000 USD in purchase protection. This badge also appears throughout the internet wherever Google lists your business, products or services such as Google search engine and Google Shopping.

Google Shopping

Google Shopping enables your products to appear on Google's main search results page and under the Shopping option on Google search engine. This function can be activated in your Google Merchant account. It is not a free service, the more you pay, the more visibility your product will have under relevant search results.

Google Alerts

Google Alerts enables you to list words you wish to receive alerts for when they are mentioned on the internet. Each time the word is used you will receive an email with links to the feature or article. You can select the frequency of alerts such as daily, weekly or monthly. You can monitor where your name, your business name, competitor's and client's names are being mentioned. You can also list key industry words, events, technology or even current affair topics you wish to keep up-to-date on.

Local Inventory Ads

This feature connects shoppers to local stores that have the inventory in stock that they are looking for. Shoppers search online for products and based on their location, Google search recommends product listings through ads. Shoppers can compare products from different stores and review that store's wider catalogue of products, seeing availability in real-time. Shoppers can then choose to purchase online or go in person to that local store to see the physical product.

6. Connect on social media

Social media has revolutionised the way businesses engage with customers and humans engage with each other. This evolution is still unfolding as technology continues to advance. Social media can be very effective if handled correctly and it's activities can provide long-lasting results. If prospect customers like your page or follow you, they are quite likely to stick with you for many years to come.

Social proof has become very important for most businesses. Prospect customers often check the social media pages of businesses to validate their authenticity, to see if customers have positive things to say and if there are a lot of people engaging with the business. Prospects are seeking up-to-date validation that you are who you say you are and can deliver what you promise. Social media helps businesses to provide this evidence. Such validation can gain businesses instant trust and rapport with new prospects and thus an edge over competitors. Social media also provides a great avenue for businesses to build brand awareness, find prospects and build relationships. Businesses not only gain access to the users who subscribe to their page, but also to their friends, family, colleagues and associates.

The opposite can be said for poor social media presence. Pages with few likes, shares or comments, gives businesses a bad image. It says that your business does not take time or interest in its social community and that your operations are lacking. Businesses must therefore maintain a positive presence on social media.

New social media platforms are constantly being introduced. Sometimes it's difficult to know which ones to use. Recent trends have also taught us that social media platforms are becoming more segmented by audience demographics and interests. According to Jones, *"A clue as to why this is happening comes from a study completed back in 2012 by the email marketing company, Exact Target. They found that people were beginning to 'segment' their communications, showing preferences for the kind of communication they wanted to receive from specific channels....they use Facebook to communicate with friends, text messaging to keep in touch with family, Twitter to chat to work colleagues and so on. Email as a channel is being seen much more as a business tool, the place where we get communications from brands"* (Graham Jones, 2015). We recommend that you use the top 3 social media platforms that your target audience are using. To select the most appropriate platform, you must have a clear profile of your target audience demographics, the platforms they use and what each platform has to offer. In this chapter we will discuss the main social media platforms that exist and their key features.

Most social media platforms share similar features such as a profile page with the ability to brand or customise, access to join wider communities in order to network and connect with other users. The option to follow users with whom you share similar interests, a celebrity or public figure you wish to keep up-to-date with. Users are able to share information with other users in the form of images, info-graphics, videos, audio and text. Users can direct message (DM) other users in their network and connect their accounts so that when something is posted on one platform such as Twitter, the same post will automatically appear on Pinterest and Facebook. Some social media platforms have different verbs to describe an activity that is unique to that platform, for example you tweet on Twitter and you pin on Pinterest. Each social media platform has its own brand, the way it operates, feels and the way users perceive it. Because of these variables, different user demographics are attracted to different social media platforms. That's why it's important to customise your communication and activity according to the social media platform you are on and the users you are interacting with.

Most social media platforms enable you to provide a brief summary of your business, a link to your website, email address, phone number, etc. Ensure that you are providing the same consistent information in the same format across all your platforms. For example, use the same brand name without abbreviations. This makes it easier for users to find you and it eliminates possible confusion about your business name. Use your business name as your url across all your pages, to make your business name more easy to find and SEO friendly. Social media is a great way to optimise your content for search engines. It is advisable to follow like-minded people or businesses within your niche so that algorithms will group you with that niche and recommend you to users when other similar businesses are being recommended.

Be mindful of your brand on social media. Ensure that your page looks attractive and professional to enable your brand to be taken seriously. The brand you project in your office, on your website, through your marketing material, should also be consistent in all your other communications, including your social media. The visual themes, company colours, logo and tone of communication should be consistent on your images, info-graphics, blogs and video content. By maintaining consistency in all these areas, you will ensure that visitors are not confused when your content is shared or when they interact with you. A solid, consistent brand presence will create instant recognition and propagate further awareness.

Social media platforms care about their community and the activities they get up to. Their goal is to grow their membership and generate a heightened level of engagement as a means to appease sponsors. Therefore they favour and promote account users who help them to achieve their goals. It's important to be human, personable, professional and interactive in order to nurture and connect with your audience. Be consistent in posting regularly, not everyone will be online every day, so those who miss your posts today, may catch another one of your posts tomorrow. The more visible you are to audiences, the more likely they are to remember you. You can stay connected at all times by downloading social media apps to your smart phone, tablet or iPad. This will enable you to interact when you are on-the-go - whilst you are waiting for a flight, sitting on a train, standing in line, or having lunch. If you are actively engaging and sharing on social media you will develop online relationships. There are different recommended times to post and frequencies of posts for each social media platform. RankAbsolute.com can provide you with analytical tools to identify the most opportune times *(see list of Resourceful Websites at RankAbsolute.com/link)*.

Don't ignore users online, in the same way you would hopefully not ignore prospects in your store, or office. If someone writes a message to you, respond to them timely. Show gratitude for their positive comments, apologise for their negative experiences and provide further support where there is opportunity. If you interact with users in this manner they will know you are paying attention to them and value your service.

Many individuals and businesses develop bad practices to grow their social media following, such as the "follow/ unfollow" tactic, especially on platforms such as Twitter, Instagram and Pinterest. This tactic no longer works, as new developments in algorithms will penalise you for such spam-like activities and, worse-case scenario, cause your account to be suspended. Social media platforms don't like unnatural, repetitive, robot-like activities. Another bad tactic individuals and businesses use is to purchase likes and followers from hacking websites. This gains them a mass of random followers, with profiles that often appear spammy. It's also obvious to many social media users which accounts purchased their followers, as their volume of subscribers don't demonstrate much interest in their brand and their vast amount of "likes" don't correlate to the poor level of comments or interaction on their page.

14 tactics to grow your following

A large social media following, where users are sharing, liking, interacting and commenting can make new prospects feel that they have been missing out on something special that others already know about. A large following also means that you have access to more leads that you can convert to customers. That's why numbers matter. There are many legitimate means for you to grow your social media following. We have listed a few below:

1. Pull in **contacts from your email list**. This is an instant means to gain audiences who are already familiar with you or your brand. If you have been proactive as a business, you

should have developed a substantial list from networking at events and subscribers on your website, at the very least, you could even start with friends, family and your local community.

2. **Cross promote on social media**. Allowing users to know you have a presence on other social media platforms will encourage them to join you on other platforms also. After all, many users tend to have accounts across multiple social media platforms.

3. Include your social media addresses on all your **marketing material** - flyers, business cards, complementary slips, letter heads, etc. As a means to prompt recipients to join your social media pages.

4. **Build alliances** with other businesses that are not in direct competition with you. Businesses that target the same customer demographic as your business, but offer non-competitive products and services. For example a gym could collaborate with a company providing a healthy energy drink. They are both targeting a health-conscious market but are not direct competitors.

You could collaborate on discount packages that are exclusive to referral customers, in exchange for advertising via each other's social media. This tactic can also be applied to email marketing and websites. For example, when a visitor signs up for a newsletter on your alliances website, another window appears offering them your service at a discount if they sign up to you also. Likewise your alliance could run a similar campaign on your website, enabling you both to benefit from each other's lead generation activities. One such example of this is Gumtree and Habitat. When you send a query to someone renting an apartment on Gumtree, another window appears offering you an exclusive discount with Habitat.

5. Provide a unique, **one-off discount** for users who subscribe to your social media pages. You can promote this offer on your website banner, social media banners and other marketing material. Once users subscribe, you can direct message (DM) them a unique code to present at check-out.

6. When you **meet new prospects** at events and exchange business cards, you could send them an email requesting them to join you on your various social media platforms and likewise you join them on theirs.

7. By using follow, share buttons or widgets on your website to **integrate your social media platforms**, you will enable website visitors to recognise that you have a presence on social media and engage with you accordingly.

8. Like influential bloggers mentioned in chapter 4, you can also **connect with social media influencers** in your industry. Firstly identify who they are, how they operate and their core target demographics. If these results complement your brand and campaign activities, you could offer them some type of incentive, whether that is monetary or freebies, in exchange for promotion on their platform.

9. **Purchase advertising** on your social media platforms to promote your services and your page. If you want to know which adverts are likely to do well on each platform, you could test them out as posts first. If they generate a lot of positive reaction you can then turn them into paid advertisements.

10. **Join groups on social media platforms**. Most social media platforms have groups. By joining groups you will gain direct access to members in those groups. The more proactive you are in reaching out to group members, the more likely they are to interact with you.

11. If you do not have the labour force at hand to help you manage your digital marketing activities you could **hire a RankAbsolute.com Virtual Assistant**. Alternatively there are a host of free and for-purchase software that can help you to decrease your social media time, without decreasing your activities, by scheduling and automating your communication in advance. These services also provide statistic feedback on your post's performance and monitor your various social media platform communications. Using such services saves you from having to log into individual social media accounts, but instead control and review all platforms from one central location *(see list of Resourceful Websites at RankAbsolute.com/link)*.

12. It's important to **measure your return on investment (ROI)**. Such as how much time you are investing, how much money you are spending and your rate of conversion through each platform. According to Jarvis *"Your goals need to be SMART: Specific, Measurable, Relevant and Time-bound"* (Jackie

Jarvis, 2015). Set numeric goals that are measurable such as the amount of target audience you want your campaign to reach, the level of interaction you wish to aggregate in the form of re-tweets, re-posts, shares and comments; The amount of conversion you wish to attain (whether that is in the form of subscribers, participants or sales), your budget and allotted time-frame. By reviewing these key performance indicators (KPI), amongst others, you will be able to identify if, or where, you are wasting resources and where your resources could be utilised more effectively. Each social media also provides its own analytics; however, they tend to provide a different set of analytical tools to those with business accounts. These analytics are highly useful in helping you to monitor the performance of your page and activities. However, having a business profile may mean that you will be treated like a business and incur additional expenses along the way.

13. Develop a **social media calendar** that ties in with your overall marketing activities. This schedule should include all the important industry dates and tie together all forms of communication, creating a cohesive, synchronised marketing effort.

14. Social media provides a great way for you to look outside of your business and see what is happening socially, in the wider world. It also gives you access to **study your clients** and prospects. To effectively target your prospects, your activities on social media should be geared towards them. It's not about what you want to tell them. It's about what they want to hear from you, in order to give you the response you desire. Think

from their perspective as to how they might respond when they see your post(s).

Promotional content about your business is not likely to get as much shares, likes or comments as much as emotional content that is inspirational, shocking, amusing or educational. When persons share posts on social media they do so to draw attention to themselves. Their aim is also to nurture their relationships and to forge greater connections with other users. If your content is successful at connecting with users on their level, users will gladly expose your business to their network of friends, family and colleagues.

We have compiled a list of some of the major forerunners in social media, outlining some of their unique features and how you can use these platforms to engage prospects.

Facebook

Facebook is still recognised as the most important social media platform although we have seen major changes in audience demographics over the past 7 years. Here are a few pointers about Facebook:

1. Facebook does not like it when users are redirected from their platform with foreign links to content such as images and videos on other websites. Instead of using Youtube videos or content from other sources, it's more effective for you to upload your files direct to Facebook. Since Facebook cannot read images or watch videos, you can promote your website

url, business logo and contact details in your actual video footage or on images you post, opposed to using live links.

2. Facebook posts have a longer shelf life than other platforms such as Twitter and Instagram. You don't need to post more than 5 times per day to be effective on Facebook.

3. You can create business pages or special interest pages and invite your followers and email contacts to join.

4. Facebook pages have a feature that informs visitors how quickly you respond to your messages. So it is important to be responsive and follow-up on your inbox queries.

5. Hashtags are not as useful on Facebook as it is on platforms such as Twitter and Instagram. Facebook works more effectively by tagging other users in your posts. However, this activity can become very annoying if the actual post has nothing to do with the person who is being tagged and if this activity is done excessively.

6. You can boost your post (a paid service) to extend its reach, but this feature does not allow you to control how you are spending your money. It's more effective to create an ad from an existing post that has already proven effective in reaching target audiences.

7. Facebook live streaming enables you to create greater real-time interaction with your followers. You can advise your followers on Facebook, other social media platforms and email database, as to when you will be going live to maximise your

audience reach. Be sure to highlight what your live stream topics will be about and ensure your topic is something audiences will be interested in.

8. Facebook instant messenger enables you to send instant messages to other members who are online. Users who are currently online will be highlighted by a green dot beside their profile on your instant messenger list. If users are not online at the same time, they will see your message the next time they sign in. Or, depending on their alert settings, they could receive an email notification.

9. Facebook phone and video calls were a strategic move to capitalise on the mobile messenger app market and is gradually proving to be effective. Facebook phone and video calls enables you to make free calls to Facebook members. The great thing is that you have access to call persons who are on Facebook who you want direct instant access to, but do not have their phone numbers. Its free and it does not require you to divulge your personal phone number. Facebook phone calls are only compatible with mobile devices through their messenger app, whilst Facebook video calls are powered by Skype, requiring you to download a plugin.

10. There are a variety of privacy settings, giving you a great deal of control over your Facebook profile, such as whether the general public can find you through search engines, what information users can access and who is able to view your posts. Your privacy settings can be targeted at specific individuals, all your friends or even the general public.

Twitter

Here are a few pointers about Twitter to help enhance your user experience, connection to your audiences and ultimately benefit your business:

1. Twitter is a fast moving platform, the more information you tweet, the more feedback and interest you will receive. It is not effective if you only tweet once or twice per day. To make a recognisable impact you need to tweet no less than 10 times per day.

2. Twitter has a 280 character limit for every tweet. Therefore users have to be very selective about the words they use. It is common for users to abbreviate their words in order to add more to their tweets.

3. There are now limitations on the ratio of members you can follow. Once you have acquired 2000 followers you can only follow approximately 10% of the amount of people following you.

4. You can interact with other Twitter users by following them, liking, sharing or re-tweeting their tweets, asking questions, posting interesting facts and quotes (accrediting the sources). These activities will cause other users to be curious about who you are, visit your profile and if interested, they may follow you, especially if you are following them. Such activities are more likely to be noticeable to users who do not have too many followers.

5. The use of hashtags against specific words will allow you to track the flow of communication related to that hashtag. You can make up hashtags around key topics that are important to your business to track how many users are paying attention to your content. Identify key industry topics that are trending and get involved in conversations using relevant hashtags.

6. You can organise your followers and the people you are following into groups to locate contacts more easily, such as having a group for influencers, another for media, customers etc.

7. Another way to maximise engagement and attract followers is to launch a contest on Twitter where the prize can be related to your products and services.

8. You can connect your Facebook and Instagram accounts to Twitter. This will enable you to post to them simultaneously when you post on Twitter.

Youtube

Youtube is an incredibly powerful tool because of its visual and audible capabilities, creating maximum impact on audiences, in a way that static images or text alone cannot. Owned by Google, Youtube videos tend to rank highly on search engines.

> Before signing up to Youtube identify how you are going to film and edit? How you are going to organise your content and deliver it? How long your videos are going to be? How frequent and at what times you are going to publish your

videos? What title is likely to attract the kind of viewers you are looking to attract? What key words prospects will use to find your videos? Before making a video it is important to establish what it is you want to achieve, whether that be advertising, growing subscribers and/or increasing hits to your online store.

1. It's important to consistently create engaging content on Youtube. Like all other social media platforms, new, regular content is important for engaging users and for ranking. You can keep visitors hooked on your channel with useful information in the format of a video series based on a specific topic of interest such as how-to's.

2. Youtube also functions as a search engine; Users enter key words and phrases in order to search for videos. As discussed in chapter 4, it is important to pay attention to your use of key words and phrases as you would in SEO.

3. Keep your video collection in a playlist so they will auto-play consecutively, one after the other. When persons view one of your videos, ideally you want them to watch another, followed by another and another. A second method you can use to achieve this is to put tags or captions at the end of each video (a clickable link) to recommend other videos. By using one video to advertise another, then the next video to advertise another, you will create a chain effect. This tends to be highly effective, especially in cases where one or more video(s) go viral, causing other videos in your playlist to benefit from that viral traffic.

4. Disable the *"Youtube suggested video"* feature. This is the only way to prevent irrelevant content that Youtube may suggest from appearing at the end of your video.

5. Clear branding will ensure that your videos are easily recognisable in a list of other videos. By adding your logo to your channel banner, video's content and thumbnail; you will make your content easily recognisable and distinct. Your thumbnail needs to be eye-catchy, to stand out amidst other thumbnails. Study other user's thumbnails to see what works and what doesn't. Adding your business name and url with a clear key word rich description will also drive traffic to your website. Also use a professional animated intro and outro for your videos to create a more professional appearance that enhances your brand.

6. The first 20-30 seconds are crucial to gaining audience attention. Don't make your videos too long. Create intrigue, mystery, and suspense, with the promise of something valuable in order to pull audiences in. Ensure that your video delivers what it promises.

7. Provide a call-to-action in your video. If viewers liked what they saw, they are likely to do what you request. It's tempting to list many call-to-actions. We suggest 2 or 3 most essential ones, such as *"subscribe"*, *"write a comment"* and *"give us a thumbs up"*.

8. Youtube will only allow you to customise your URL when you have achieved 100 subscribers or more, your channel is more than 30 days old, with professional banner and thumbnail.

9. Youtube algorithms pay attention to how many users watch your videos all the way to the end, write comments, select thumbs up or thumbs down, the number of subscribers you have and whether they select more videos in your channel. All these activities, if carried out, will boost each video's credibility on Youtube and on other search engines. Subscriptions on Youtube are the most important feature, because you can share your future content with subscribers more easily.

10. You can invite audiences to live video streaming sessions. This way audience can comment, ask questions and interact with you in real time as you are streaming.

11. Upload your video transcripts to enable Youtube to identify the keywords and phrases in your content for SEO purposes and also to enable them to add subtitles.

12. Do collaborations with other Youtubers that have a similar audience, views and subject interests. This will enable you to benefit from each other's audiences.

13. Comment, like and share videos from other channels within your subject area. By participating in the Youtube community, users will automatically check out your page. But don't irritate others by posting unhelpful, negative comments or self-promoting links to their page. This will only result in them deleting your comments or blocking you. Add value to their page and support their cause, in turn they may do the same for you.

14. You can increase the reach of your videos by sharing it across your social media platforms, adding it to your website, other websites, sharing it through email communication or advertising it on Youtube.

15. You can promote your products and services in a subtle, non-pushy way that does not deter from the value you are offering through your content. Such as product placement, or a brief mention at the end of your video.

16. Get your video added to the *"suggested videos"* section by having a great eye catchy thumbnail, strong title that is relevant to a specific topic and capturing viewer's attention within the first 20 seconds. Do not deceive viewers with irrelevant poor content, or they will abandon your video and distrust further videos from your channel. Provide great content that resonates with viewers. Edit to ensure your videos are concise, impactful and does not waste valuable time.

17. Each video has the length (time) on the thumbnail. Unless your video is an interesting movie, or a Tony Robinson seminar, viewers don't expect to spend 1-2 hours watching your content. Viewers have short attention spans and many distractions. So cram the value-based knowledge you wish to share within a short space of time. Youtube does not give you much clout if your video is too short. We suggest no less than 5-10 minutes.

Instagram

Instagram (owned by Facebook) grew to phenomenal success in a short space of time. Its level of celebrity endorsement, controversial images and ability to capitalise on the selfie generation spurred it's success further, creating new terms such as "Instagram-famous".

1. The timeline is where you post text, images, info-graphics and videos. You can also choose whether or not to enable comments for your posts.

2. You can create your own groups and encourage users to join as a means to gain access to direct messaging (DM) and increase engagement.

3. The tag feature enables you to tag users in your photos and videos, in a similar way to Facebook's tag feature. This will enable your content to appear in the timeline of the users you tag.

4. View other popular posts to see what kind of content on Instagram gets the most views and likes in your industry. As long as your content is engaging, interesting, of value to your followers, they won't unsubscribe from your account.

5. Instagram is more image-focused than most platforms. It is essential to make sure your images are of a high quality. Consistently post images within a specific niche or theme, e.g. if you work in travel - post travel images, if you work with animals - post animal images. Keep your image format consistent. The portrait format works best with Instagram images.

6. Be natural and conversational in the way you communicate with users. When you interact by liking, following and commenting on other user's posts, you will increase your followers.

7. Instagram has a feature which allows you to geotag your images. This feature amplifies your post within your location. Thus enabling your content to stand out amongst users in your locality. This feature is very effective because other users often like to feel connected and aware of what is happening around them.

8. The stories feature gives your content a 24 hour window of exposure through a prominent position on your follower's pages. If you publish every day on Instagram stories, you will get more recognition from your followers. You can also increase engagement by adding a poll with a yes/no option for other users to vote.

9. Instagram's live video streaming enables you to have a direct conversation with your followers in real-time. You can also save your Instagram live streams to the stories feature to give them a further boost.

10. The use of hashtags enables you to expose posts to wider audiences. Adding a hashtag automatically categories your content according to the hashtags you select. Carefully select the most appropriate hashtags that will gain you the correct audience to grow your prospects. You have a maximum allowance of 30 hashtags for each post. When you search for a hashtag on Instagram a drop down menu appears highlighting

how popular that hashtag is. Don't use hashtags that are extremely popular or your post will be lost in the crowd. Instead, use hashtags that are reasonably popular and are directly connected to your core target audience.

11. A post is most valuable within the first hour it is launched. Gain as much engagement for your post as possible within that first hour. This will ensure your post ranks high with each hashtag and is visible to other Instagram users.

12. You can run a loop giveaway. This is when a group of Instagram accounts work together to give away prizes such as money, clothes, tickets, products and services. Each Instagram account encourages their followers to participate in different activities on their profiles, which could include liking posts, joining profiles, writing posts, etc. Participants complete tasks on different profiles until they are directed back to the first account where they started. This enables participating accounts to increase their followers and engagement levels, using the followers of other accounts. Do not include too many accounts in the giveaway or participants could get tired of too many activities. Also ensure that the prizes are very enticing.

13. You can collaborate with other Instagram users to trade video shout-outs. This will enable you to gain exposure to their loyal followers and vice versa.

LinkedIn

Owned by Microsoft, LinkedIn is the largest social network for business professionals. It specialises in human resources, with user's profiled by their skills, experience and expertise. LinkedIn is probably the most under-estimated social media platform, because many users still have not yet come to grips with it's capabilities. LinkedIn is often thought of as a glorified digital curriculum vitae for job seekers. However, as a formal, more conservative platform, it is also great for networking and attracting your ideal prospects. LinkedIn works best when you optimise your profile to be a solution provider, specialising in a particular industry niche, with the ability to solve the problems of your target market. Here are a few tips on how you can make the most out of your LinkedIn profile:

1. Your headline is where you introduce yourself professionally. It has a 120 character limit and may be a great place to include your website url.

2. Like most social media platforms you are able to customise your LinkedIn url.

3. Profiles on LinkedIn, like other social media platforms, rank high on search engine result pages (SERP).

4. There are sections to add your work experience, academic history, areas of expertise, awards, certificates and references. It's easier for users to read and more effective if you use bullet points. Also write your key accomplishments and achievements in first person narrative.

5. LinkedIn is the ideal place to identify key persons in an organisation you wish to connect to and reach out to them. You can also target users in your local area, somewhere physically accessible so that you can create an opportunity to

meet them in person, whether that is to arrange a meeting or invite them to an event.

6. You can use groups to connect with other users on LinkedIn. You can join up to 50 groups and create up to 10 of your own. Within these 10 groups you can create 20 subgroups. You can send an auto message to someone the moment they join your group. You can offer them a lead magnet such as a free report, sample of your book or invitation to a free event, as a means to get them to submit their details to you. It's important to have a large group, with tens and thousands of members that you can email direct. Having a group enables you to make announcements to all your members at the press of a button. When you are a member of a group you gain special privileges that you would not have otherwise, such as the ability to direct message (DM) the members of the group you are in. Each time you send a DM this message appears in user's email accounts, depending on their account settings.

7. When you communicate on LinkedIn ensure that your messages are professional and customised to each individual. You can do this by mentioning specific things from their profile. This increases the likelihood of getting a positive response.

8. LinkedIn is not as fast-paced as other social media platforms. Users do not often spend continuous time on this platform. Therefore when you send direct messages (DM) it may take a while for users to respond.

9. LinkedIn has a referral system where your network can click a button to refer you and provide a supporting statement about your expertise. Just like other social media platforms, images stand out more than words alone. According to Doris Day: *"people hear what they see"*. Be exceptional in your posts and comments in order to stand out, gain user's interest and approval.

Pinterest

Pinterest is not for all types of businesses, it works best with businesses that showcase products or services such as cooking, fashion, graphic design and interior design. This platform is also used as a search engine, in a similar way to Youtube, Google or Bing. Likened to how key words and phrases are important to search engines, they are also important to Pinterest. Pinterest is also a great place to shop and seek advice.

1. You can categorise yourself or your business based on your interests, industry or the interest of your prospects. This will enable you or your business to be referred by Pinterest to other users based on the categories you select.

2. Similar to Twitter and Instagram you can follow other users. If they like your posts or the way you interact, they may choose to follow you.

3. Like Instagram, Pinterest is image-driven. Pinterest requires thought-provoking or stunning images to draw user's attention. Pinterest is designed for large vertical images and works most effective when images have text (info-graphics). Pinterest

enables you to pin images and view images other users have pinned. Re-pinning accelerates the popularity of a pin, whilst click-throughs increases the popularity of a blog. The pins that get a lot of re-pins are info-graphics that give readers an incentive to click through. Pinterest has strict copyright rules. Use images for which you have copyrights. There are stock photography websites where you can acquire free and for - purchase theme based photographs *(see list of Resourceful Websites at RankAabsolute.com/link)*.

4. Users browse Pinterest at lightning speed, with a downward scroll action. You may have less than a second to catch their attention. Therefore clever info-graphics can entice users to stop and read your pin. Ensure all your images have a visually, easy to recognise theme. Your info-graphic must create mystery, intrigue and curiosity, whilst your blog or website must reveal the bigger story attached to the pin. Tell user's something they don't know, solve a problem, give users a reason to bookmark your pin and come back to it later. How-to's and lists are effective on Pinterest.

5. If you delete a blog or webpage with pins, you must remove the pin link on Pinterest. Pinterest penalises accounts with errors such as broken links.

Blogging sites (Tumblr/ Blogger/ Wordpress)

Tumblr, Blogger (owned by Google) and Wordpress, are a few leading blog-based social media platforms. Tumblr, having a less corporate appeal than the others, is used by users with wider, more varied interests. Here are a few tips that are common amongst most blogging platforms.

1. When you share other user's blogs, it will appear on your wall so that your followers can read it. The person whom the blog belongs to will also be alerted that you have re-blogged or shared their blog. In turn they may do the same for your blogs.

2. Only put quality original content on blogs. With eye catchy titles, images, info-graphics and/ or videos.

3. As mentioned in chapter 4, when we spoke about SEO content, key words, phrases, meta tags, backlinks, along with quality, engaging, long-form content are all essential to gain high SEO ranking for your blog.

4. Focus your blog on a niche topic and surround yourself with a network of bloggers with the same interest. To find other bloggers in your industry you can search for them by their niche blog topics, using the search icon. Then identify the authors of the content and follow them.

5. The more followers you have on your page and the more you interact, the greater the likelihood that others will see your content, like it and re-blog it. The more people re-blog your blog, the greater the potential will be for it to go viral.

6. On platforms such as Tumblr you can use RSS automated emails, crafted to your select template, to send out email/newsletters each time you create a new blog post.

TAKE ACTION:

- *Review the social media platforms you present your business on, asking yourself the following questions - Are you using too many platforms? Which platforms are the most effective and least effective? Are your social media leads converting to sales? How can you improve your performance on each platform?*

- *Using the analytical tools available on each platform review how prospects are interacting with you. What time of the day are they most active? What kind of posts do they respond to? If you do not have business accounts on these platforms we, at RankAbsolute.com have provided 3rd party analytical tools that will help you to analyse your social media pages (see list of Resourceful Websites at RankAbsolute.com/link).*

- *Develop a content calendar, with a schedule of posts for each platform, ensuring your content also coincides with industry relevant events. You can then begin to schedule future posts using the automated 3rd party websites we have provided.*

7. Mobile Technology

Most of us can still remember when mobile phones came on the market. Our new-found ability to make and receive calls whilst walking down the road seemed far-fetched, until it happened. Then another game changer - the smart phone, enabling us to connect to the internet, stream online, record videos and audio, play games, check emails, use GPS to find locations and so much more. Mobile messenger apps soon exceeded social media platforms in terms of subscribers and levels of engagement. The exponential growth of these apps was fuelled by user's desire to avoid high call and text charges both locally and internationally. We have also seen a slow increase in text message marketing which is still relatively under-utilised. In this chapter we will explore mobile technology capabilities.

Periscope/ Meerkat (Video streaming apps)

Periscope and Meerkat were revolutionary back in 2015 when they were introduced to the market with their unique selling point of live streaming. Now many social media platforms have this inbuilt live streaming functionality. The ability to live streaming is about being present and in the moment.

1. These mobile apps work in tandem with Twitter or Facebook, having the ability to pull in contacts. When you click the play button on Periscope all your Twitter followers are notified and are able to re-tweet the broadcast to their followers. You also have the option not to alert your Twitter followers.

CHAPTER 7: Mobile Technology

2. You are able to have one-to-one encounters with other users, including celebrities, asking them questions in real time.

3. When someone streams live you can see what they are up to in a very organic, unfiltered, free-styling manner. You can stream live events, host live question and answer sessions, showcase products and services such as interior designing, construction, music, muscle building, etc. You have access to see all kinds of random live streams. You too can live stream to the world or privately to a few and limit the amount of people that can comment on your video. You can also broadcast your location while streaming, receive alerts when others are live, access broadcasts taking place around the world, in real time; Award streams with hearts and other emoji, save your video, edit it and use it on other social media platforms to maximise your potential audience. Another way to achieve this is to schedule live streams in advance.

4. Similar to social media, you can search for users, follow users, send and receive messages. You can also categorise your topics using hashtags.

5. Hearts are what Periscopes users award videos to attribute value to them. You can run contests and giveaways for hearts and shares. When you give someone a heart, the more likely their post is to appear on the leader board and be broadcasted to a wider audience. You can end your broadcasts with a call-to-action, such as encouraging viewers to award your stream with hearts.

Snapchat

Snapchat has a younger demographic than most mobile platforms. There are not many business interactions on Snapchat. But there are some opportunities for branding.

1. Snapchat is mainly driven by photos and video stories captured directly through Snapchat's camera feature.

2. You can customise the screen with emojis, text, decorations, filters etc.

3. There is a feature called geotag which enables you to show your location and for you to know where all your contacts are in real time. As long as their Snapchat is switched on.

4. Likened to other mobile messenger apps, you can send text messages, images and videos.

5. There is a *"discover section"* where you can see posts by various brands.

6. You can add contacts by user name, phone contacts, Snapcode or even proximity. If someone is physically next to you, you can both switch on Snapchat to search for each other's user names.

Mobile Messenger Apps

The main mobile messenger apps on the market include WhatsApp, WeChat, Facebook Messenger, Viber, Skype, Line, Kik*, Blackberry

Messenger and KakaoTalk. The following bullet points highlight some of their main features:

1. WhatsApp is the current leader, whilst WeChat is it's close rival competitor, with its largest market being China.

2. It is illegal to use WhatsApp commercially. This does not, however, hinder companies from using WhatsApp for customer service purposes and the media. Whilst other apps such as WeChat are used more commercially.

3. Text messages, images, info-graphics, videos and audio recordings can be sent via mobile messenger apps.

4. Mobile messenger apps are ergonomically clean, easy to use and their communication is designed to be more private, direct and instant.

5. Some apps such as WhatsApp have a group function, which is great for events, special interest groups and for instant messaging the masses. Because everyone can see the messages in groups, they are best used amongst users who know each other, opposed to more formal business usage.

6. Mobile messenger apps do not require much information to set up an account, in the way that social media platforms do. All that is required is a phone number.

Text Message Marketing

Text Message Conversion Rate

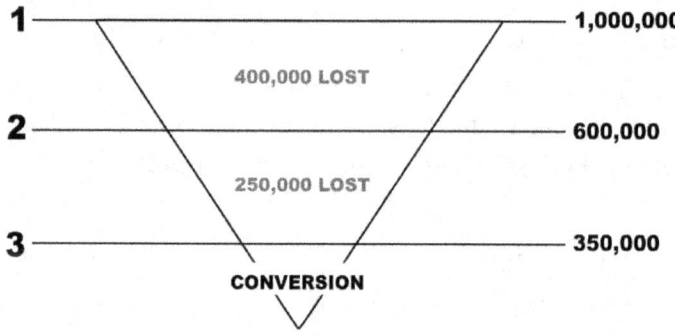

1. 1,000,000 prospects targeted via text messages. 400,000 prospects lost due to factors such as incorrect phone numbers.

2. 600,000 prospects receive text message. 250,000 lost prospects due to factors such as un-opened texts, distractions or not interested.

3. 350,000 (35%) prospects respond positively by responding to the text.

Fig 3. Text Message Conversion Rate

If email marketing has a high conversion rate of up to 20%, it's safe to say that text message marketing's conversion rates are likely to be 35% or more, due to its directness and having less barriers such as filters. Text message marketing is increasingly becoming today, the phenomena that email marketing was 10 years ago, yet still relatively under-utilised. Text messaging has a far higher open rate (OR) than emails. Most people check their text messages almost instantly after receiving them. Text marketing may not be suitable for all types of businesses such as B2B wholesale or manufacturing. However, this form of marketing is highly effective in B2C situations where communication with the masses is required. Texting as a form of business communication has been commonly used by medical centres and dental practices, as a means to up-date patients on appointments; Television/cable programmes for poll voting, fast food companies with promo codes on flyers to encourage participants to opt-in and various companies for short questionnaires. Texting is increasingly being used by online platforms such as social media, email accounts, banking or government websites to provide security, authentication, verification and access.

Similar to email marketing, text message communication requires approval by the recipient. Where gdpr (general data protection regulation) governs general data, tcp (telephone consumer protection) governs phones. If using text message marketing here are a few tips to consider.

1. Ranking second to the phone feature, the texting feature is highly prominent on all mobile phone devices.

2. Texting is a personal mode of communication, which is void of spam filters. Through text messages we anticipate communication from those who are close to us such as friends, family and colleagues. We are therefore very receptive to this mode of communication. So it's important to make your communication tactile and friendly.

3. People are a little more guarded about submitting their phone numbers than email addresses because of the personal nature of phones and the lack of protection against spam and unwanted communication. That's why it's important to offer a substantial incentive to prospects and customers such as prize draws, in order to gain their participation.

4. Text messaging is a great way to run contests and polling. You can add text promo codes to your campaigns, marketing material, business card etc.

5. Similar to email marketing, once you have captured phone numbers through opt-in campaigns, you can schedule and automate messages, segment contacts and broadcast to the masses at one click of a button. Then monitor the feedback of your campaign performance.

6. Currently there is less competition from businesses using mobile phone communication, opposed to email, social media and other forms of digital marketing.

7. Recipients will not automatically know who you are so it's important for text communication to include your business name, along with a special offer, expiry date, call-to-action

and an option to opt-out of future communication. You are also able to attach links to images, audio, videos and websites.

8. Because text messages are limited in content and format they are quick, short, easy to read, and as such, they usually generate quick responses.

9. Text marketing can be more expensive than other digital formats, depending on the network provider or the geographic location of recipients. Because of this expense it's highly important to use this method only where the return on investment (ROI) has a high potential.

10. Like all other forms of contact, text message marketing is a great means to build a relationship with prospects and customers. Especially when you send special birthday texts offering a discount of gift.

Social media platforms and mobile messenger apps are not entirely reliable. It's important to understand that these platforms allow you to use their services. You may work hard to acquire an audience on these platforms, but ultimately this network does not belong to you. These platforms have the power to dictate how you interact with their users. They can lock you out of your account, go bankrupt and shut down activities, causing you to lose all the contacts you have gained. It is therefore essential that once you have established a fully functional system of generating leads via social media, mobile messenger apps and other sources, you must get hold of mobile phone numbers and email addresses. We will be discussing email marketing in the following chapter.

TAKE ACTION:

- *Identify what mobile messenger apps you can use to interact with your prospects and customers?*

- *How can mobile messenger apps integrate with your website?*

- *Is text marketing effective and feasible for your business?*

8. Effective Email Marketing

Email Marketing Conversion Rate

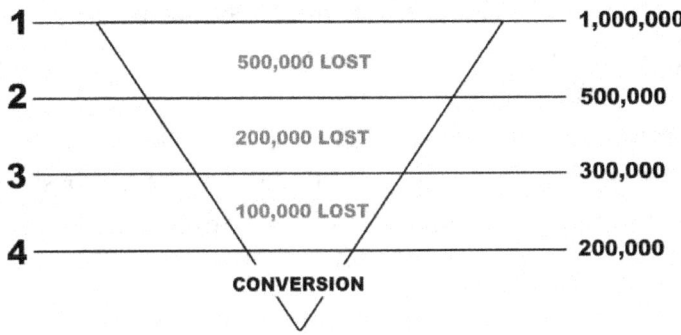

1. 1,000,000 prospects targeted via email messages. 500,000 prospects lost due to factors such as bounced emails, incorrect email addresses, spam, junk and promotional filters.

2. 500,000 prospects progress to inboxes. 200,000 lost prospects due to factors such unappealing subject heading, unopened emails, distractions or not interested.

3. 300,000 are curious enough to open their emails to find out more information. 100,000 prospects are lost due to factors such as being distracted, procrastination, price sensitive or not interested in the product or service.

1. 200, 000 (20%) successful conversions. These prospects either provide their details or purchase a product or service.

Fig 4. Email Marketing Conversion Rate

In an age where birth is given to a new social media platform every other month, email is one of the most consistent, reliable and effective form of contact. As mentioned previously, with social media you don't own your followers or your page. Therefore, building your email database is one of the most important and empowering means to establish and secure a long-term connection with your target audience. Email marketing is one of few forms of digital contact you can truly own, with the flexibility to format and brand your communication the way you want to. Although email software may be required, you can export your contact database in a csv or xls file format and use it elsewhere at any time, because they are your contacts.

Email marketing is one of the most dominant forms of digital marketing activities. As highlighted in chapter 2, according to Jones (2015) it has one of the highest conversion rates of 20%. Email marketing also has a perceived level of formality. People rely on emails to do business. The inbox is where employers and prospect employers communicate with employees and prospect employees. The email is where you receive your bill notifications (paperless billing), promotions from your choice brands, notifications from the bank, confirmations of payments for purchases you have made and its delivery status up-dates. People are receptive to email marketing because they can control it through unsubscribing or junk mail filters. Emails are a great way for businesses to announce a sales promotion, event, product launch or share company news. If you don't use email marketing, you are literally loosing prospect customers and ultimately losing money.

Since you have already put all the necessary work into your social media marketing, enabling you to build and nurture relationships with your followers; building a relationship with your email network should not be too difficult. Those who subscribe to your social media platforms are already acquainted with what you do and what you have to offer. Via email you are now able to offer them more value with greater freedom in how you wish to format your communication and what information you wish to communicate. Before you can achieve this, the first thing you need to do is to gather your email database.

To grow your email list, you can collect email addresses when you network at events, seminars, business meetings or exhibitions. If you identify key information through dialogue with prospects in person you can let your prospect know that you wish to keep in touch with them and that you have some useful tips that may help them to solve their dilemma. You can also collect email contacts via phone queries, sales and abandoned shopping carts on your website. Another method is to create an incentive for your social media audiences to submit their email addresses to you such as basic opt-in forms that can also be placed on your website. Another effective method is to create a landing page, a page used to draw audiences from your social media or other online locations with a lead magnet. A lead magnet is an incentive (something of value) that incites prospects to click your landing page and submit their information. Landing pages will be discussed in more detail in chapter 9.

Having successfully collected prospect's email addresses, you can use email software to store, maintain and monitor your database, create attractive custom branded email newsletters and execute campaigns. This software will also provide analytical feedback for each campaign, such as how many recipients opened your email, their geographic location, the device they used and what links they clicked on. You can integrate your social media by adding logos and live links. You can segment your mailing list according to variables that are important for both your business and your target audience such as location, country, age group and sex. Depending on the size of your database, email marketing may be free or low-cost. We have listed several email software services that can help you to manage your mailing list *(see list of Resourceful Websites at RankAbsolute.com/link)*

Another useful function of email software is the ability to automate your messages. A sequence of emails can be scheduled to go out to recipients, every day, once per week, or once per month after they have subscribed. This sequence of emails can strategically introduce you and your business to new prospects and build rapport with them over time; the ultimate objective being to acquire sales. As this process is fully automated, once you have put in the initial research and strategic thought to organise your communication, you no longer have to be present. You can simply sit back and observe the sales process take effect, monitoring and adding the occasional tweaks here and there, if required. Initially this process may require some trial and error, based on the unique nature of your business and the type of customers. At first it may also seem painstakingly time consuming but in the long run it will prove highly effective.

In accordance with gdpr guidelines it is important to inform recipients of how frequent you will communicate with them, the type of communication you will be sending and provide the option to unsubscribe. Gdpr regulation ensures that subscribers who opt-in to your mailing list actually want to receive your emails. Knowing they have this level of assurance and empowerment makes subscribers more receptive to your communication. Based on the fact that your database was gathered from individuals who willingly submitted their email to you, your initial email contact with them is likely to be received warmly, especially if you contact them soon after acquiring their details. The benefits derived from this "warm" approach, is that you are less likely to suffer rejection after rejection, low blows to your self-esteem and wasted time and resources. Once your audience become familiar with your communication and what you have to offer, you will eventually be able to identify which subscribers are likely to be serious and eliminate non-responsive subscribers from your list. It is important to communicate with the subscribers who genuinely want to receive your communication. This ensures that your contacts are high quality prospects that are likely to increase your percentage of open rates (OR) and sale conversion. Initially the goal is to gain their permission and then their continued acceptance of your email communications. So don't engage in hard-sell techniques from the get-go.

Your email not only has to win the approval of recipients but also junk mail and promotional filters. That's why it's important to make your early email communications seem more informal and friendly. Similar to emails you would send to a colleague or associate, (void of promotional images, videos and too many links), use simple plain text. Once subscribers accept your email communication with ease, you have entered into what Godin (2002) describes as "permission marketing".

Increasing your open rate (OR)

It's important to differentiate your email communication from inbox clutter with an effective email strategy. Email services such as Gmail and Yahoo look for open rates (OR) and scan email contents to determine if they will place select emails into junk or promotional filters. Therefore its crucial, for the continued success of your email communications, for you to increase your open rates (OR). To achieve this there are 4 main areas to place great emphasis on in your email communication. These are - 1. subject line, 2. the personalisation of each message, 3. appearance and content of your message and 4. the call-to-action.

1. Subject line

Once the recipient is acquainted with you, (by way of meeting you at an event, connecting with you on social media or using your website) and they are anticipating your email communication, it's time to implement your email strategy. Without a strong subject line, the email content and supporting strategy are not worthwhile. Ensure your subject line is short, effective and relates to the rest of your email. A subject line starting with the word *"hey..."* is an informal, chatty approach, which sounds like a friend so recipients may want to read on to find out more. But it is not very professional. So whether you use such an approach will depend on your line of business and target audience.

Have you ever received emails with the following words? *"You will love this"..."Have you seen this?"*. The word *"this"* is often used as it conceals, adds intrigue and is a good word to lure audiences and invoke curiosity. Email subjects such as these are now often used by spammers because of their known effectiveness. In a B2B context we recommended that you use words that are more distinctly recognisable to you and your recipient. You may wish to try - *"Was nice to meet you at..."* This is a more gentle, chatty and specific approach for a subject line. It implies that you have already made physical contact with your recipient. *"Here are the... you requested"*, is also highly specific and likely to prompt the recipient to open your email because they are receiving something they requested. Yet depending on the content's call-to-action it may not garner a quick or engaging response as it is not a question. At the very least, if the email content is useful you are likely to receive a *"Thank you"*, in return.

Alternatively you could try - *"Are you still struggling with ....?"*, This is a direct question and depending on the subject matter it's also very specific. Being that this it is a question, it is also likely to prompt a response. The rate at which such an email is opened or responded to will also depend on what the initial physical encounter was like; whether the person took a strong interest in you or your business and the level of perceived interest in what you are offering.

The above subject lines were mainly geared towards B2B communication. If engaging B2C prospects you are likely to have received their email from a website newsletter sign-up, opt-in form, or an abandoned shopping cart. In such cases your subject line could be a friendly *"Thank your signing up, we have exciting news..."* or *"Welcome to our exclusive..."*, Although this is more generic, it can help to make prospects feel they are a part of something special or exclusive.

2. Personalisation

This is your opportunity to build likability and trust as an expert in your field. If your email is impersonal, spammy or promotional, filters will prevent your emails from reaching inboxes. The more personal your emails are, the more likely they are to reach their destination and be opened by your target recipients.

You should address your recipients by their actual name opposed to a generic "Sir/ Madam". Recipients don't want to feel like another contact in your database. At the same time you should not overuse your recipient's name in the email content. This too can begin to sound spammy or unnatural. Don't make your communication self-indulgent, simply speaking about yourself, your products or your business. Neither be vague, dismissive and impersonal. Tune into your recipients by sharing your personality. Be honest, vulnerable, trust-worthy, transparent and most of all valuable. When you are honest, you connect with people and they connect with you. It's important to create this sense of knowing and trust whether in a B2B or B2C context. According to Jones: *"Very few of us are prepared to buy things when we do not trust the seller. Furthermore, few people are prepared to pay for things they believe are unethical or sold without ethical principles."* (Graham Jones, 2015).

In a B2B situation you can attempt to offer further personalisation by tailoring your email to your recipient's specific interests. If you are offering a service that involves something visual, you can embed the recipients brand in your communication, with a customised diagram or sample of work, so they can foresee what it is you are able to offer them. Relate your message to what your recipient does and is interested in, without putting pressure on them to call or meet you. Messages requesting a call-to-action such as *"click here"* or *"download"* is easier to achieve once you have your recipient's attention.

3. Appearance and Content

Whatever subject headings you choose to use, ensure that the first sentence of your email is strong and raises curiosity. This is highly important because most recipients can see a preview of your message before they open the actual email. Some recipients rely on the subject heading and the strength of this first sentence to determine how they prioritise each message in their inbox. It's important to understand that each recipient could have 100 to 300 unopened emails in their inbox; your message must therefore compete for their attention.

Your content should deliver what you promised in the subject. For example, in a B2B context, if you used a subject heading such as - "Here are the ... tactics you requested". A strong opening sentence could be, *"Clients who used these... tactics increased their sales by ...% in their first year".* It's important to add a call-to-action or question to further the dialogue. A call-to-action could be - *"Let me know if you find the attachment useful, we have further resources that could help you to…".* Alternatively if you used a subject heading such as *"Are you still struggling with ....?",* a strong opening sentence could be - *"If so, I have a few proven techniques that you may find effective".* These short email messages are direct, to the point and just enabled you to ignite a dialogue.

In a B2C situation where your subject line is less personal your emphasis needs to focus more on promotional incentives such as free giveaways. Recipients tend to favour non time-consuming messages. Long emails often intimidate recipients, who are likely to save them for later, leave them with an unread highlight in order to address them at a more opportune moment; ultimately creating opportunity for recipients to procrastinate. Recipients also enjoy receiving positive, helpful information. Conduct research on your prospects to enable you to tailor your messages accordingly.

Gradually you will develop a relationship with recipients of your newsletters. Your recipient's lack of response does not always mean that they are not paying attention. It could simply mean that they are not yet in a position to respond. But your continued efforts - providing small tips, tricks and industry know-hows, will enable you to establish yourself as their go-to expert the moment the opportunity presents itself. Jarvis described such an experience, sharing: *"She called me out of the blue and it was as if we had a relationship already. My tips over the years had built her trust in my knowledge and she was at the point where she was ready to buy more."* (Jackie Jarvis, 2015)

Our suggested contents for emails are quite vague and are only mere examples of how you can use words to generate intrigue and initiate dialogue. It's up to you to provide the actual value behind the words. What's important is that you don't give everything away at once, use your email dialogue as a window of opportunity to learn more about your recipients through questions and answers, ultimately winning them over with your level of expertise. Offer them some amount of free advice. If they want more, you can offer your products or services as ultimate solutions to their problems.

This personable, friendly, chatty approach is more likely to increase the open rates (OR) of your emails, create a relationship and open channels of communication about your products and services. With other forms of warm email dialogue sparked from an abandoned shopping cart, email query, or a successful sale, it is important to keep this communication going. You may also be able to up-sell similar or complementary products and services. If you are a B2B service, your dialogue could easily progress to a telephone conversation, a coffee, or a meeting at either yours or your client's office. Whatever is necessary to secure that prospect. Where B2C is concerned, you will seek to keep communications online and less personal.

Many emails don't automatically download images. Activating image downloads can be difficult on small mobile phone screens. If you choose to use images, ensure that they have been customised for both desktop and mobile devices with alt text. Also ensure that the words you use are significant enough to work without the aid of images. It's important to keep the same format in every email e.g. layout, colour scheme and language. Following the same theme in every email will enable you to build brand familiarity and rapport with prospects across all communication platforms. Your email format should have some similarity to your website or landing page. Your prospects shouldn't feel as if they have arrived somewhere that is completely unfamiliar or alien to them when they click through to your website or landing page.

The success of your email communication depends on your technique as much as your overall attitude towards business. Customers are clever and they will see right through you. According to Jarvis:… *"…the desire to help your customers* succeed is as much an attitude of mind as it is a set of actions. If you are clearly focused upon your customers' success, they will pick up on that and reward you accordingly."* (Jackie Jarvis, 2015). We encourage you to submerge yourself unequivocally in the customer experience, dedicating yourself to delivering the solutions your customers are seeking.

4. Call-to-action

One of the obvious differences between your call-to action in emails opposed to social media and other platforms is that you no longer need to acquire email addresses. You have your audience exactly where you need them and now your communication is focussed on building a relationship and introducing them to your products and services in order to secure sales.

Once you have developed a relationship with prospects and you are ready to entice them with freebies, you can begin to include call-to-actions in your emails. Ensure your call-to-action is distinct and easily recognisable in your email. You could use a different colour, size, font, bold, italics, a button or even a directional cue to help prospects focus on what you want them to do.

The particular call-to-action you use will depend on the type of products and services you have to offer and whether you have a B2B or B2C operation. As such, your email and landing page will have a similar call-to-action. For example your email may prompt prospects to visit your landing page with a call-to-action such as *"Get your free copy – click here",* whilst the call-to-action on your actual landing page could say - *"Download your free copy - click here"*. Try different call-to-actions to see what works best for your audience.

Another great way to entice recipients to take immediate action is by using scarcity and a limited time offer. For example you could let prospects know that this special offer is limited to a specific number e.g. 200 giveaways at a special discounted rate, for only three days. This will create a sense of urgency and a need to take action right away or risk losing out on a one-time special offer.

Send test emails to yourself to review its appearance and to check that all relevant information has been included. Read your email aloud as though you were the recipient. Hearing your message out loud will enable you to objectively judge it's likely impact. You can also send a test email to colleagues, employees, friends or a sample audience, opposed to your entire mailing list, to test the likely impact. If you don't see a strong response you need to revise your email strategy, identify its weak areas and adjust accordingly.

Analyse your campaigns, paying attention to open rates (OR) and click through rates (CTR), to see how prospects are responding. If they don't respond well, this could mean that your subject headings are not effective enough, it's the incorrect time of day, or day of the week for your communication, or maybe junk filters are sending your emails direct to junk mail boxes. Try not to lose un-subscribers before finding out 1. Why they are unsubscribing and 2. If they are simply price sensitive. If you believe that they would be hooked once they give your product or service a try, you may wish to present a unique one-off discount offer to entice them further. You can present this offer at the point where a prospect is about to unsubscribe.

Be consistent in sending emails. Sales are often acquired as a result of repetitive behaviour. Large brands spend millions on repetitive TV, radio and print advertising, because they recognise the significance of building brand awareness. If a prospect remembers a brand, they are more likely to select it from the shelf at the super market. Likewise it's important to apply this technique to advertisements on other formats such as social media and email. Sometimes visitors won't remember how they came across your brand or your website, but the very fact that there is some type of familiarity, increases the likelihood of them purchasing from you. The frequency of your email depends on the products and services you have to offer. If your product is seasonal (for Christmas, Easter etc.) there is no need to email all year round. Your communication would seem irrelevant to recipients and you will lose subscribers.

TAKE ACTION:

- *Develop an email marketing strategy by first identifying how you will acquire warm email leads.*

- *Sign up to an email marketing software service (see list of Resourceful Websites at RankAbsolute.com/link). Using the techniques described above, develop a sequence of email communication with effective subject heading, opening sentence, personalisation and call-to-action.*

- *Your sequence of emails will introduce you and your business to prospects then build familiarity to a point where you can follow-up with sales emails.*

- *Test your email sequence on a small sample to gage its effectiveness - tweaking and adjusting where necessary.*

9. Landing Pages

A landing page is a page designated to generate leads or sales for a campaign. The core elements of a landing page often includes a persuasive heading, subheading, call-to-action, opt-in form, attractive background image or info-graphic, a 3 to 4 step guide and a specific lead magnet (free giveaway), designed to drive prospects to make a purchase or to submit their data. Prospects are usually directed to a landing page by links on social media, through PPC advertising on search engines, websites and email communication. One campaign may have multiple landing pages to appease various prospects, segment markets or to monitor and manage where traffic is being generated from. There are two types of landing pages; lead generation landing pages for the purpose of gaining information or contact details and click-through landing pages used in e-commerce to drive traffic to an online store or check-out.

The perceived value to customers of what you are offering will determine the effectiveness of your landing page. According to Jarvis: *"If you can uncover the fundamental outcomes and values that your customers are looking for, you will have much greater influence in your sales conversations."… "The clearer you are about the value you offer, the more able you will be to influence your potential customers positively. To have the greatest chances of success, your messaging should be targeted at the specific needs and interests of your target audience."* (Jackie Jarvis, 2015). The fundamental principle always comes back to having a clear understanding of your target market, their pain point and being able to provide a valid solution. Before designing your landing page identify the most compelling elements prospects need in order to take action.

Trust is the first thing you are selling to prospects. It is essential to eliminate any form of apprehension, delay or uncertainty. To achieve this you can include a comment or testimonial section displaying genuine feedback from customers who have used your products and services. This kind of social proof helps to reassure prospects of the value you are offering and lower their sense of perceived risk. According to Jones; *"Buying something involves risk - we risk making the wrong purchase, spending money unnecessarily, for instance. So, we seek to minimise that risk"*... *"Hence, the more information available via the web, the more research people will do in order to satisfy their inner need for risk reduction."* (Graham Jones, 2015). Save prospects the research and delay in decision-making by providing the information they need.

To increase the effectiveness of your landing page you can include a short persuasive video, make your opt-in form short, requesting only essential information; Likened to your email communication, reiterate your limited time offer, scarcity and a strong value proposition to create a sense of urgency, thus enhancing the volume and speed of your conversion. To maximise conversion, landing pages must be simple and focused, dedicated to one specific call-to-action (CTA); with limited distractions, entirely focused on the conversion process.

TAKE ACTION:

- *Develop a landing page using the techniques mentioned above - attractive appearance, small opt-in form, attractive background a lead magnet, etc.*

- *Test your landing page on a small sample to see how effective it is. Tweak and adjust where necessary to improve the performance.*

10. Retaining customers

It is more time consuming and expensive to acquire new customers than it is to keep current ones. Jones supports this idea stating: *"If companies were to spend more time looking after the needs of their existing customers, they would be able to reduce their costs of customer acquisition…"* (Graham Jones, 2015)

Understanding customers

To retain customers you must first understand as much as you can about them. What motivates your customers to choose your products or services above that of your competitor's? Is it simply convenience because of your geographic location or opening times, the easy-to-use layout of your physical or online store; The perceived emotional attributes of your brand; Your wide range of products and services, affordable prices, enticing promotions or friendly well-informed staff? Once you have identified what motivates your customers, you can ensure that you sustain or enhance the qualities that appeal to them in order to maintain your competitive edge and secure your long-term customer base. It is crucial to pay attention to these perceived values because if they are altered in the wrong way your company could risk losing customers to competitors. What customers like and dislike is equally important. If you understand what customers dislike, you can also decrease the likelihood of them leaving you for the competition. Likewise it is also vitally important to understand what the competition is offering that you do not offer.

You can gather information about your customers through useful statistical feedback from online analytical tools such as Google Analytics or social media analytics. You can also conduct surveys, questionnaires or collate valuable information over a period of time through your own customer relationship management (CRM) software. CRM capabilities are essential for businesses. Effective CRM systems will enable you to collect detailed information about each customer such as their contact details, sales history, personal preferences, previous communications (via email, phone calls, social media and meetings); Record, report and share this information across the company. Empowering you to manage and nurture your customer relationships.

Having detailed information about your customers will enable you to save money, time and resources. For example if you were able to identify where your customers are coming from, e.g. a 3rd party website such as an online directory, you will be able to identify which promotional avenues are working best for you, cut back on efforts through less effective mediums and increase efforts where they work best.

Since your current customers are already familiar with you, they are more likely to increase their spending with you. It is therefore easier for you to up-sell your products and services to them. Jones makes mention of this, stating: *"Knowing your customer thoroughly means you can anticipate their requirements. It means you can act in a consultative way and, as a result, sell more to them. Excellent customer knowledge means more sales. Getting to know your customers as well as you possibly can produce financial rewards."* (Graham Jones, 2015). Jarvis also supports this idea stating: *"Taking the time to understand your existing customer's changing needs will ensure that you are there with solutions before they think of using anyone else. It is important that you keep talking to your customers as they can be a great source of information for you."* (Jackie Jarvis, 2015)

Loyalty schemes

Loyalty or membership schemes are an effective way for businesses to entice prospects and encourage a long-term relationship with current customers by showing appreciation to them for their loyalty. The very notion of a loyalty scheme implies that if a customer stays with your company long-term they will gain more aggregated advantages, rewards, discounts, or even prestige as a valid customer. As a part of a loyalty or membership scheme customers can collect points each time they shop, receive exclusive discounts, free products or services, special seasonal offers or even invitations to exclusive events.

Going the extra mile

In this competitive climate you have to be prepared to go the extra mile to exceed customer's expectations. An ability to be innovative and think outside the box will enable you to maintain a competitive edge. It's not just about acquiring that sale and then seeking the next. It's important to build and maintain a relationship no matter what kind of business you are operating. According to Jarvis: *"Continuing to communicate with your customer after they have finished doing business with you will ensure that your customers know you care. It will also leave the door open for future business"* (Jackie Jarvis, 2015). You can create opportunities to make positive contact with customers such as sending annual greeting cards at

Christmas, birthdays, anniversaries and other special occasions. Surprising customers with a special discount or unexpected gift. Such communication is warmly received by customers.

You can add a more personal touch, with the occasional phone call, email or letter, thanking customers for their customs and offering them an exclusive gift or treat the next time they visit your store or office. By acknowledging and treating customers like individuals you will make them feel special and valued. I once heard a saying: *"customers may not remember what they bought from you, but they are likely to remember how you made them feel"*. Focus on detail, be considerate and thoughtful, deliver the products and services you promise in a timely, professional manner. Create an unbeatable, exceptional, memorable customer service. Whilst keeping an eye on the competition to maintain your competitive edge.

TAKE ACTION:

- *Develop a mental image of what your key target audience look like, their core demographic makeup, their interests and their lifestyle. Write a list of their characteristics, then a list of the things they like about your products and services along with a list of the things they may not like.*

- *Analyse what your competitors are offering and the incentives they use to entice prospects.*

- *Based on the information you have acquired, write a list of initiatives you can take to increase their loyalty to your business, brands, products or services.*

11. Referrals and Reviews

Nothing beats word of mouth when promoting your business. Our most prominent form of word of mouth are referrals and reviews. Referrals are when customers directly entice other prospects to acquire your products or services. Whilst reviews are what customers have to say or write about their experiences using your products and services. Because referrals and reviews come direct from customers who have experienced using your products or services, it is a great way to establish immediate trust and rapport with prospects who have never heard of your business. This immediate trust can then be converted into immediate sales. Referrals and reviews help prospect customers to minimise the possibility of making a bad purchase. To gain a referral or review you must earn it by providing an exceptional experience that customers are willing to speak highly of. As long as you provide a very good product or service and your customers are happy, do not hesitate to ask for referrals or reviews.

Referrals are a great way to acquire ideal customers. If your existing customer refers someone to your business, chances are that they are likely to refer someone from their network, who shares similar tastes, income and lifestyle. If using a referral scheme, it is important to make the process quick and easy for your customers. Traditionally referrals were based on the strength of a business's relationship with their customers and required some form of direct personal communication between the referrer and the referee, which posed a barrier for some businesses who, understandably, felt it was intrusive to request this of their customers. However, the advent of social media changed all this. Facebook built its entire empire on referrals as each Facebook member was able to send his/her contacts requests through their email list. Eventually everyone had several Facebook requests in their inbox and it became difficult to ignore. This method was quick, did not require a personal conversation, instead just a couple clicks of a button.

The One Plus One (OPO) mobile phone's empire started through referrals. You could only become a customer by receiving an invitation from a customer. This was quite revolutionary for a mobile phone company. The energy company, Bulb, in the UK, offers their customers a monetary reward for successful referrals. Both the referrer and the referee receive £50 towards their bill. Other methods of acquiring referrals include exclusive membership cards that offer access to an exclusive club.

The strength of one referral may be enough to secure a sale, but several consistent positive reviews are usually required to provide that level of certainty. Reviews are not as personal and direct as referrals and therefore not as powerful. Traditionally reviews were found in magazines, trade publications and newspapers which gave them a lot of clout. Now they are typically found on Google review, Trustpilot, websites and social media platforms. Likened to referrals, businesses can directly ask their customers for reviews or via a thank you email - adding a small link and note stating *"If you like our product/ service feel free to let others know by writing a quick review using the link below"*. If a business is confident in the level of feedback they will receive they should ensure that they are listed on review sites. However, if there is any discrepancy as to the quality of feedback they are likely to receive, they may wish to gather feedback in a more direct, discreet manner, by conducting surveys, questionnaires or collecting feedback through online forms and via email. Based on the type of questions you ask, you could gain valuable detailed insight highlighting areas where you are underperforming as well as confirmation on where you are performing well.

Bad reviews shine in a cloud of great reviews. But don't ignore them. Respond to them right away with an apology, explanation and a suitable remedy that will appease the disgruntled customer and reassure prospects who may have seen the review. Many customers are willing to overlook short-falls when recompensed with an effective follow-up such as a genuine heart-felt apology and, if necessary, a form of compensation. It lets prospects know that even though you make mistakes, you take full responsibility and resolve situations. This kind of follow-up is likely to help you win their confidence, in spite of any negative set-back. Some sites enable users to edit their reviews. If someone wrote a bad review, you can resolve the situation in a manner that guilt's the reviewer into retracting or changing their review. Also be sure to respond to good reviews. Let reviewers know that you have seen and appreciate their feedback.

TAKE ACTION:

- *Identify where you could improve your performance with your customers.*

- If you feel confident about your performance, *subscribe to review and referral websites.*

- *If you are not so confident try to find ways to improve your services. A great way to do this is through anonymous, confidential questionnaires.*

12. Get free publicity

Most businesses hire a professional marketing agency with access to agency-only PR tools, contact information and editorial calendars of various media outlets; With the expertise to pitch ideas that will generate a media buzz. The following are tips on how you can generate some media buzz of your own:

1. **Approaching various media direct**. This has the lowest potential returns, but with a certain amount of creativity you could gain some attention. One such example of creativity and ingenuity was AirBnB. In 2008 when AirBed & Breakfast was launched, a team of 2 (Brian Chesky and Joe Gebba) were living in a shared apartment, unemployed and struggling financially. They attempted several business ideas that failed. But their desperate need to make their rent payment led them to host guests in their own home at a time when a local convention was taking place and there was a shortage of rental accommodation. They hosted 3 people, made cool friends and paid their rent.

   They went on to develop the business concept by adding a developer to their team. They struggled to get their business model off the ground. One of the challenges were convincing investors that ordinary people would be willing to share their homes with strangers. Another challenge was generating publicity to draw participants to their website. They came up with the idea of capitalising on the national elections by making collectable breakfast cereals, one called *"Obama O's, the Cereal of Change"* and *"Cap'n McCain's,*

A Maverick in Every Bite". This idea took off, each cereal retailed at $40 USD each, generating approximately $30K. They sent their cereals to media houses who thought it was worthy of a feature. This publicity enabled them to generate the seed capital they needed (Fortune Magazine, 2017).

2. It's easy to think that your story is very important, simply because it is important to your business. But you need to be far more objective, your story needs to be **newsworthy** for your target audience and the media outlet you are approaching. The best approach is to identify what your target audience interests are. If your story has a genuine appeal to audiences, then media houses are likely to be interested. Media houses need to captivate their audiences in order to appease their sponsors. So its within their best interest to follow-up on stories that are likely to create an impact.

3. Publish your press release stories to **news feed websites** *(see list of Resourceful Websites at RankAbsolute.com/link)*. Don't send out mass generic press releases to random journalists. That is the perfect way to be ignored. Journalists need original exclusive material.

4. You can **speak at events** (for free) where the press is likely to attend. Not only will this build your profile as an expert in your industry, but you may be able to generate some free press coverage in the form of local press and or industry trade publications. After your event you can approach journalists to provide them with all the necessary incentives and encouragement to publish an article about you. This

may include your contact details, a quote, images, or even a recording of the event.

5. Be a **guest speaker on radio shows**. Ensure that you maximise these engagement opportunities by obtaining video and photograph coverage so that you can post these to your social media platforms, further helping to build your profile. We can recommend a great website with useful radio contacts to get you started *(see list of Resourceful Websites at RankAbsolute.com/link).*

6. Create a **publicity stunt** that draws the attention of local and/or international media. The type of publicity stunt will depend on the type of products/services you offer and your target audience. Fashion house *United Colors of Bennetton,* was well-known in the late 90's for their outlandish publicity stunts, often in the form of prominently located large billboard adverts with provocative, controversial subject maters such as racism and HIV.

7. Create **promotional videos**. These could be videos you capture of your speaking engagements or even vblogs. These can be posted to your Youtube channel and shared across social media.

8. You can **sponsor an event**. The larger, more prestigious or controversial the event, the more media attention it is likely to garner. Your logo signposted throughout the event, displayed on the promotional material and highlighted in news coverage will secure your publicity feature.

There is a saying that *"no publicity is bad publicity"*. As highlighted in this chapter, some businesses are willing to risk causing offence with their message in order to generate awareness of their brand. It's up to you to decide how you wish audiences to perceive you and your brand.

TAKE ACTION:

- *If you have a sizeable budget, approach a marketing agency, such as RankAbsolute.com to engage their PR services.*

- *If you do not have a sizeable budget start to investigate potential newsworthy stories about your business, or publicity stunts that can create a media buzz.*

- *Research a list of industry specific events that you can speak at, develop a bio and make a proposition to event organisers.*

- *Identify radio stations that may be interested in your story or professional tips you have to offer and contact them for a feature. Ensure that they target your audience demographics.*

- *Identify key industry publications that you may be able to publish an article in. Review the subject matters they write about, develop your feature and submit it to their editor with a brief bio about yourself.*

13. The future of Digital Marketing

Let's take a look at some of the digital trends that have revolutionised our world and some of the likely trends that are unfolding. Over the past 20 years we have seen the successful introduction of the smart phone, teaching us to swipe and tap, online universities, facilitating remote studies, a decrease in physical stores as retail moves online. Businesses cut costs when they retail online and customers get cheaper prices when they purchase online. We have also witnessed the growth of a sharing economy with services such as Uber and AirBnb. Never before in history has it been easier to launch, operate and promote a business, with little to no capital.

Loss of Anonymity

Social media has stripped back the walls of anonymity, enabling us to research the life of a romantic interest, a prospect employee, a competitor or prospect client. With access to see their photos, photos of their associates and loved ones, read communications and observe their interactions with others. You can even see their interests, groups they are a member of and a brief history of their education and employment - stalking has never been easier. This stripping away of anonymity has brought us back to a sense of community where we are no longer complete strangers. Likewise businesses that operate within our community are represented by individuals that we can identify and have access to. Originally this is what the business place was all about, the community - the corner shop, the mum and pop store, the butcher, the ice cream man and the bakery. Although we no longer have a physical sense of this small community in many cases, businesses are now able to forge this kind of community relationship online.

Sharing Economy

This sense of community continues to expand through the concept of the sharing economy. Who could have thought that strangers would open their doors to other strangers whether that is to share their couch, book their room, apartment or even their entire house. Thanks to AirBnB, Couchsurfing and other similar platforms. Digital technology has also made it legal to hitch-hike again as individuals are now able to book rides in stranger's cars, thanks to the likes of Blablacar.com and Liftshare.com. We anticipate that the sharing economy will continue to open doors for entrepreneurs and individuals to share their lives and resources with others, earn side incomes and receive more accessible service solutions. In times of greater economic challenges people tend to cut more corners, join forces and become more resourceful. Digital sales also thrive in an economic downturn. As stated by Jones: *"...online retail sales have continued to grow throughout the economic troubles of the post-recessionary world." Yet during the five years after 2008, traditional sales fell in many sectors"* (Graham Jones, 2015).

Business Alliances

In order to compete with this sharing economy and provide more competitive services, it is quite likely that businesses will form more alliances and take part in cross-promotional activities as a means to capitalise on each other's services, share each other's clients, promote each other's brand and services, impact wider markets, cut costs and in some cases, offer greater value to end consumers.

Mobile Technology

Mobile technology will continue to dominate the digital sphere as people are constantly on-the-go. Mobile platforms will take over larger desktops and laptops completely, with the use of ad-on monitors and keyboards for users who need wider screens for work purposes. Platforms such as WhatsApp and Skype will then seamlessly integrate into your computer technology and become more compatible with websites. Without requiring your formal phone number users can call you direct from their computer or mobile device if they have a query; Thus further increasing our level of instant accessibility and level of engagement.

Algorithms

Currently algorithms are making search engines increasingly adaptable to logical human behaviour. As more individuals and businesses become knowledgeable about gaining high-level search engine ranking, the stakes will increase as algorithms will continue to seek more stringent ways to evaluate and validate users. We anticipate that an even greater onus will be placed on the level of content authority and authorship.

Beyond the scope of social media and mobile messenger apps, algorithms will continue to solve more of our everyday problems; finding quicker, easier solutions and enabling artificial intelligence to interact with humans in a natural manner.

Voice Technology

It's questionable whether consumers will take to voice activated appliances and smart home technology quickly. But voice technology has already proven highly effective with mobile phone, automated voice machines, media devices and entertainment. Technology such as Alexia, Seri and Google Assistant are paving the way. According to digital marketing expert, Gary Vaynerchuk (2017), voice technology will replace writing, because its faster and more natural to talk than it is to write. Already people are conducting a lot of voice searches. It is therefore necessary for us to start considering how voice technology can be integrated into our digital marketing capabilities to create greater efficiency for us and our consumers.

The law

The internet may have levelled the play field for new businesses to enter the market with little to no capital. But digital technology brings its own set of challenges. With so much of our lives in digital format, there is a need to protect our online information through legislations and greater online policing. These same useful advancements have opened us up to unregulated content, exposing children to adult material; Threats to our security with online banking and other personal information being preyed upon by hackers. These are just a few disadvantages of our new digital world.

According to Jones: *"... as the researchers point out, unethical behaviour is more likely online than in the 'real world'. Human interaction, including the assessment of body language and other non-verbal communication, means that unethical sales behaviour is much less common face to face because it can so easily be spotted. Online, of course, with no tone of voice or facial expressions to analyse, it is much more difficult to spot unethical behaviour. You might therefore reasonably expect unethical sales to be more prevalent online. Combine this with relative anonymity of the internet and you can see there is a recipe for unethical sales people to find a market online."* (Graham Jones, 2015)

The moderately successful, yet subtle introduction of gdpr is paving the way for more online law enforcement. The subtle enforcement of ssl certificates, without which users may receive site warnings, making them uncomfortable about placing their credit card details on your website, is gradually changing businesses approach to retailing online and customers approach to purchasing online. We are all looking for more security. As such we will continue to see an increased level of enforcement through the companies that provide services that enable us to have a presence online. All businesses operating on the World Wide Web must purchase hosting and register their domain name from a provider. It is through these channels that laws can be enforced.

14. Conclusion

Welcome to the exciting world of digital marketing. Digital technology is dynamic. Change always seems daunting at first, however, digital advancements are not a force to be reckoned with. Don't be so caught up in the day-to-day activities of "business as usual" that you fail to take into account the new developments in your business environment. With more sales transactions taking place online, it is important for you and your business to have a significant strategic online presence.

Having read this book, we hope you now understand some of the main digital resources at your disposal and how they can benefit your business, such as search engines, email marketing, social media, Google, blogging, websites and mobile technology. As mentioned, in addition to what we have discussed, there are also industry-specific digital platforms: The retail industry has Amazon.com and Shopify.com; The vacation industry has TripAdvisor.com and Booking.com; The music industry has Spotify.com and Pandora.com; The accommodation industry has Rightmove.com and Zoopla.com, so the list goes on. Each platform has it's unique advantages and disadvantages. Their relevance is based on your marketing mix, industry and the unique nature of your business.

We used the sales funnel as the basis for your overall digital marketing strategy ensuring that your activities are geared towards maximising conversion. We presented tactics to help you develop a highly effective customer-orientated, SEO and mobile friendly website. We explained the evolving landscape of social media, how audiences are now segmenting their communication, how to select the most effective social media platforms to present your business on, locate and attract niche audiences, automate your social media campaigns in advance with pre-planned content calendars and secure long-term prospects regardless of the social media platform they use.

We explained how to increase the acceptance and open rates (OR) of your email communication by overcoming barriers such as junk mail and promotional filters; the type of messages that agitate eyeballs and create immediate action; Along with ways your businesses can create dominance and influence online. We looked at the important role mobile technology plays in the digital marketing sphere and ways to integrate mobile technology into your marketing activities; How to gain warm sales leads that are more positively accepted, opposed to cold sales leads that are prone to rejection. Amongst other topics, we also looked at the future trends of digital technology such as the growth of voice technology, the sharing economy and increased legislations.

Digital marketing has many benefits, whether you are seeking to raise awareness, strengthen your sales process, identify prospects, connect with them and convert them into repeat customers. Digital marketing is the most cost effective, measurable form of marketing that exists. It's also a great means for you to create maximum impact with little input if you know what you are doing. Otherwise you can waste hours, days and months not getting anywhere. Each digital medium requires a specific method of customer-oriented engagement to achieve a successful outcome. If you don't follow the required protocol for each platform, it's highly unlikely that you will achieve the outcome you desire. It is therefore important to be strategic with your digital marketing activities in order to make the most out of your time and resources.

Capitalism and innovation means that anything that can become digital is likely to become digital. Digital is fast, cost-effective, resourceful and highly accessible. The digital trend setters of the future are companies and individuals most skilled and innovative in their ability to generate a buzz, establish a recognisable brand and connect to audience's emotions in a meaningful way.

Yet this window of opportunity won't last forever. As the saying goes - *"Nothing good lasts forever"* and *"All good things must come to an end"*. Increased legislations will create more safety but limit our capabilities. That's why it's important to make use of the vast opportunities at hand today. It's time to get digital, if you want to make big profits with little effort.

15. References

Books

Ashton, R (2003) *Copywriting in a week, be a great copywrite in seven simple steps*, Hodder Education. An Machete UK Company.

Booms, B., H., and Bitner, M., J., (1981). Marketing strategies and organization structures for service firms, in Donnelly, J., H., and George, W., R., (eds). Marketing of Services. Chicago: American Marketing Association.

Chaffey D and Ellis-Chadwick, F (2016) *Digital Marketing: Strategy, Implementation and Practice,* Sixth Edition, Pearson Education Limited

Godin, S (2002) Permission Marketing: Turning Strangers into Friends, and Friends into Customers, Simon & Schuster

Jarvis, J (2015) *Quick Wins in sales and Marketing, 50 inspiring ideas to promote and grow your business*, Robinson, London

Jones, G (2015) *Sales Genuis: 40 insights from the science of selling*, Hodder & Stoughton. A Machete UK company

Kourdi, J (2007) Business on a Shoestring - Surviving a downturn, building a successful business without breaking the bank, A & C Black Publishers Ltd

Smith, PR and Chaffey, D (2005) *eMarketing eXcellence: The Heart of eBusiness*, Second Edition, Elsevier Ltd

Videos

Fortune Magazine (2017) Interview With Airbnb CEO Brian Chesky. Retrieved October 4, 2018 from <https://www.youtube.com/watch?v=GFMeuSIhIYg>

Lever Interactive (2017) Digital Marketing Trends for 2018 event with Lever Interactive and Google. Retrieved October 14, 2018 from <https://www.youtube.com/watch?v=ZRX_PJIEQnQ>

Patel, N (2017) 6 BEST Digital Marketing Tools to Grow Your Business Online. Retrieved June 14, 2018 from <https://www.youtube.com/watch?v=Uar2hXRrckY>

Patel, N (2017) 7 Landing Page Hacks That'll Double YourSales | AWasia 2017. Retrieved June 14, 2018 from <https://www.youtube.com/watch?v=FpM578W3ORw>

Vaynerchuk, G (2017) Incredible 106 Minutes on the Future of Entrepreneurship and Technology. Retrieved October 17, 2018 from https://www.youtube.com/watch?v=hka_rdo_7MY

Websites

Erskine, R (2018) Google+ Never Really Stood A Chance (And That's Okay), Retrieved October 22, 2018 from <https://www.forbes.com/sites/ryanerskine/2018/10/15/google-neverreally-stood-achance-and-thats-okay/#2c4f18bb4c7c>

ABOUT RANK ABSOLUTE

At Rank Absolute we help our clients to achieve their business goals by enhancing their visibility and conversion rates through digital marketing.

We specialise in GDPR compliance, SEO, social media, email marketing, mobile marketing, graphic design, web development, app development and so much more.

FREE DOWNLOAD

Download list of Resourceful Websites from:
rankabsolute.com/link
using the following code:

128767

NEWSLETTER SIGN UP

www.rankabsolute.com

Sign up to our newsletter to join our RANK EXCLUSIVE CLUB and receive exclusive tips, reports, industry up-dates and invitations to events such as seminars and training courses.

JOIN US ON SOCIAL MEDIA

 @rankabsolute

www.ingramcontent.com/pod-product-compliance
Lightning Source LLC
Chambersburg PA
CBHW051318220526
45468CB00004B/1401